T0157626

My LIFE with RITA,

THE
Love of My Life

Jim Booksh

iUniverse, Inc.
New York   Bloomington

iUniverse books may be ordered through booksellers or by contacting:

iUniverse
1663 Liberty Drive
Bloomington, IN 47403
www.iuniverse.com
1-800-Authors (1-800-288-4677)

ISBN: 978-1-4401-7658-6 (sc)
ISBN: 978-1-4401-7659-3 (ebook)

Printed in the United States of America

iUniverse rev. date: 04/06/2010

Dedication

My Life with Rita is dedicated to my loving wife, Rita Larcade Booksh, who was my inspiration and the one I was so in love with for the fifty-eight plus years we were together. I hope my narration of how sweet and loving she was is appropriately promulgated by my writings. Without her, I do believe I would not have been as successful in life. She remains my solitary gal, and I sincerely believe my life with her was a preview of what heaven is. If my life on earth with her was not heavenly, then I cannot imagine how the hereafter can be better since I have already had a wonderful preview of life hereafter.

I also dedicate this book to Suzanna Alleman, who was instrumental in inspiring me to write my memories and even located a writing class to ensure I did it correctly. She was also helpful in correcting some writings and attempted to engrain in my mind how beneficial a computer could be in writing it. Without her expertise and patience, it is doubtful this writing could have been completed. My thanks to her are well- earned.

Introduction

For more than fifty-eight years, I lived with the love of my life: my wife, Rita Leona Larcade Booksh. Those years, I believe, have been my time in heaven. She was the smiling will behind my working life, which brought us to so many wonderful places in this magnificent world. She was the drive behind my working life and believed that her man made the best decisions and provided the best for their marriage during his working life. She seldom disagreed with my decisions and thoughts. I would have not changed our way of life for anything. I may have changed one move, but then we would have missed an opportunity for an exciting assignment overseas.

Oh, how I loved her! How beautiful she was! What made her so lovely? Was it something that could be named and analyzed? No, I don't believe so. Perhaps the Lord, using simple lines and with one stroke, drew an arc around her, instilling in her that magical beauty, beautiful brunette hair, brown eyes, gorgeous complexion, wonderful personality, and pleasing temperament, all woven together with a smile for everyone.

I wish to summarize our many years of married life and how Rita was able to care for me, her aged mother, and my brother. I will also describe how, in later years, I took care of her when she was afflicted with a dreaded disease. The doctors and I searched for medicines to help her. There were few available then, and I do not believe the situation has changed. We used only what I called "experimental medicines" to fight her problem. Her pain may have been eased, but my wife was never cured.

I hope my attempt to narrate some of the details will make pleasant reading. The many moves we made to parts of the world could have been taxing for some; however, my life with my understanding partner was altogether wonderful. Rita helped me in a manner that improved our lives and made living as happy and enjoyable as it was.

CHAPTER 1

RITA'S LIFE IN RAYNE

Rita, a native of Rayne, Louisiana, was born in 1922 in neighboring Lafayette Parish where her father was a farmer. I do not believe she would have ever enjoyed farm life. When I met her twenty-four years later, she was afraid of, or at least disliked farm animals. In their fenced backyard in Rayne, Rita's father had a cow, a horse, and a barn. Rita had no desire to open the gate, get near the barn or either animal. She once told me, "The animals are for my father and brother to take care of. I have no desire to be near them."

I must say that the cow gave the richest milk I had ever tasted. After milking, the milk was stored in a large crock bowl in one of those early iceboxes that was kept cold with block ice brought from a horse-drawn wagon. The ice was made at the local downtown icehouse. Electric refrigerators were on the market, but the Larcades had not purchased one at the time; they simply used ice made by Rita's great-grandfather who happened to own the local icehouse.

When the milk crock was removed from the icebox, there was usually an inch or more of cream on top of the milk. Getting that much cream in a paper carton with one's milk is a thing of the past! If anyone wants rich cream these days, it has to be purchased separately.

In the 1930s, Rayne was a town of approximately four-thousand inhabitants, composed principally of two races: Caucasian and black. The area was settled by foreigners who migrated from the foreign lands of Europe, including Germany, France, England, and Italy. Others came from Africa and Mexico. Cajun French and southern English are still spoken there to this day. The area is known as the prairie of southwest Louisiana, and rice cultivation was and still is the principle crop because of the level plains and elevation. Because of the many rice fields that require irrigation, Rayne has become the Frog Capital of Louisiana. The rice fields have become a perfect breeding ground for them. Similarly, the nearby town of Crowley has become known as the Rice Capital of the World because of the many rice farms and mills in the vicinity.

Rita's mother's ancestors migrated from eastern Germany in the early 1800s and settled in what became the German settlement of Robert's Cove, a few miles from Rayne. Her mother, Sepha Gossen, was a first-generation child. Similarly, Rita's father was also a first-generation American of French ancestry. After farming, he became a successful insurance agent in Rayne, earning the trust of many in town and in the surrounding parishes.

Rita grew up in Rayne and was known by her nickname, "Tee-ta." Because she had a problem pronouncing her name Rita, Tee-ta became her name to most of her friends and relatives! She attended Rayne High School where she graduated in 1939. She became rice queen for the Rice Festival that year because of her beauty which lived with her so many years. Even in her eighties people marveled at how well she looked. Her brunet hair did not have a spec of gray hair nor were there blemishes on that beautiful face! And, of course, that smile was given to all who said hello! As a music lover, she joined the high school band as a drummer for football games, and she was a cheerleader for basketball games. Her popularity at LSU continued. During her freshmen year at the university, she was selected as a beauty queen for one of the football games. Wherever she went, she made many friends, both male and female.

CHAPTER II

Army Life: 1942 to 1946

I was born in Morgan City, Louisiana, but I lived in Plaquemine and eventually moved to Lafayette, Louisiana at age seven. I lived about thirty miles east of Rayne where I frequently went on high school dates. I never had the fortunate occasion to meet Rita. Some of my friends dated girls from Rayne, but none ever mentioned her or her name. I do believe Rita and I had similarities since we both lived on farms during our younger years. Dad, a true salesman and manager, retired from the wholesale grocery business, then bought a fifteen acre farm while my two brothers and I were in high school and later college. It can be said Rita and I were identical in our dislike for farm life. Actually, neither did my mother or her three kids.

At an LSU dance, my roommate, Fritz, introduced Rita to me. It was only a casual "hello and good-bye" introduction. I remembered the meeting, but at the time I was more interested in a Lafayette girl and commuted home each weekend to be with her. .

By the time the Japanese bombed Pearl Harbor on December 7, 1941, I had transferred from LSU to the local college in Lafayette, known then as Southwestern Louisiana Institute, now as the University of Louisiana at Lafayette. In 1940 I left LSU because of my immaturity and the mistake of moving into a" Frat House" my second year there. My folks had sold the farm and moved a block from the campus of SLI in Lafayette where I continued my college education while pursuing a degree in civil engineering. However, in June 1942, before graduating, I was drafted into World War II and sent to Fort Hood, Texas for basic training. After that I qualified for the Army Specialized Training Program (ASTP) college training and was sent to the University of West Virginia in Morgantown, West Virginia to complete my education. My schooling, however, lasted only one semester before the Army eliminated the program in 1943.

Our class was immediately assigned to the corps of engineers at Camp McCoy, Wisconsin. From there I was sent to Fort Belvoir in Virginia, near Washington DC, for training as a topographic draftsman engineer. I soon learned that dating in nearby Washington DC, with its many females, was too costly for a private's pay. One date and I was broke for the remainder of the month!

After training at Fort Belvoir, I was sent back to Camp McCoy and my 655th topographic battalion. Shortly thereafter, we were sent to Camp Polk in Louisiana for overseas training. There we were acclimated to a very hot, early summer climate. The weather did not affect me, but my poor northern friends could not take our summer heat and humidity, for they passed out like flies when we went on our many forced marches. After a quick orientation in Louisiana, we were shipped to a port near Philadelphia and finally to cool England on a merchant ship. There we became part of the European Theater of Operations and the Fifth Army.

The voyage across the Atlantic Ocean reaffirmed my decision to enlist in the Army rather than the Navy. I was seasick the entire trip. At times I felt like jumping overboard. Being bunked in the lower bowels of the crowded ship and the absence of fresh air did not help me or my many shipmates who were as sick as I. It seemed that after playing cards, the only other activity available besides KP or kitchen police as it was called in the army, was "up-chugging" along the ship's rails.

Somehow we all arrived safely in England. There we received more training while we awaited a trip into Germany where the war was being fought. In England, when we visited London, we heard an occasional German "buzz bomb." On one occasion one hit an adjourning building we were sleeping in. The explosion woke us temporarily, but we just turned over and went back to sleep. The countryside where we camped and trained was very quiet, and the English there were very friendly. It seemed the inhabitants liked the "Yanks" who had come over to save them.

Ninety days after D-day, when the Allies stormed the beaches of France at Normandy, my battalion arrived in France. Crossing the English Channel to France was the only sea travel I made aboard a ship without being seasick. At the time I was too afraid of being ambushed and strafed by German fighter planes!

From France we moved into Eastern Germany, crammed in a freight train composed of boxcars formerly used in World War I to transport ten horses or twenty crowded soldiers. It was the same arrangement for World War II. We slept on straw scattered on the floor, and because it was so crowded, we had to turn over on command, one at a time! One of our comrades, a cook, cried out on one turn: "If I have to do this again, I am going to shoot someone to get more room!" I doubt if he would have hurt anyone, but he was very perturbed that night. He may have been excited, but we just laughed it off since we had rifles but no ammunition.

Our first stop in Germany was at Mheer Castle, a small abandoned castle complete with moat, drawbridge, and towers near the Belgian border and not too far from Maastricht, Netherlands. It had been abandoned by the owners, who'd fled the country because of the war, but it was in perfect condition for a drafting company so it became our headquarters. There we performed duties fitting our training, including mapmaking, detailing maps for river crossings, adding overlays, and other topographic duties required by the Fifth Army in Germany to whom we were attached.

The castle was so large that we were able to sleep, work, and eat within its walls. It was very comfortable. One day three of us borrowed a jeep and rode into the nearby town of Aachen which had been completely bombed out. Little did we know Germans were still there! We didn't see any but heard several shots and quickly high tailed it back to our castle! From there we moved many times in the western and northern parts of Germany. We headquartered in the towns of München-Gladbach, Fulda, and Bielefeld, the last of which is the birthplace of my great-grandfather. When the war ended on May 8, 1945, we were headquartered in the town of Brandenburg, only ninety miles west of Berlin, where Hitler committed suicide.

I remember I broke my right hand in Brandenburg playing softball. A professional baseball player in our company threw his knee into my right hand as I attempted to tag him out at second base. I did not expect, nor did I receive a purple heart for the episode. Foolishly, I mailed a picture home showing my bandaged right hand. This turned into a problem with my folks. It was hard to convince them that I had not been injured by the enemy in battle; it took several letters to finally convince them it was an accident. My drafting duties, however, had to be curtailed for a short time nonetheless.

The war ended a few days later, so I lost very little time at work. After VE day, our battalion left Germany and was assigned to a redeployment camp in France several miles from Paris. We were being prepared for an early transfer to the Far East. Thank heavens the war ended after the bombing of Japan, for I doubt if I could have lived through a long journey to Japan on a troop ship. Being so near Paris was exhausting, but enjoyable for the many visits we made there celebrating the end of the war. Paris, we learned, was as beautiful as advertised.

Soon after, our battalion was again sent back into Germany and became part of the occupation forces. I spent a year there until I had accumulated enough points for a discharge and a return home to Cajun country in Lafayette. Occupation duty had not been hard at all. There were no riots, no bomb explosions, and no resistance by the locals or similar disturbances to contend with. The Germans were so happy that the war was over and that they had been liberated from Hitler's rule. All who I met were friendly and hospitable. In fact, our duties there were pleasant and almost as routine as being at home.

CHAPTER III

MEETING RITA IN 1946

In March 1946 I returned to Lafayette after my discharge from the army and began life again at home. It was great. My number one objective was to obtain an engineering degree, find a job, and continue my relationship with Mary, with whom I had communicated for three years while in the Army. There was no doubt I would finish college as soon as possible. The army had taught me that an education was of prime importance, and the GI Bill of Rights was my ticket to attending college free of charge.

My first date with Mary after returning from the war was just before lunch. I picked her up for a short ride to become reacquainted. During our meeting I realized she was not the girl I had dated before the war. It seemed that despite the old saying, her heart had not grown fonder of old Jim while he was away. We broke up before we finished lunch, and I was footloose and fancy-free. I was free to look for another girl!

Shortly thereafter, my younger brother Jack, who had served in the Air Corps during the war and was now married, asked if I was interested in dating a young lady friend of theirs, Rita from Rayne. I was game, so I said, "It is fine with me. I have no other plans."

The date was on a Sunday afternoon. We drove to Rita's home in Rayne, only thirty or so miles west of Lafayette where I met

Rita, her father and mother. After introductions we journeyed back to Lafayette and stopped at a local club, Toby's Lounge, at the four corners for cocktails and later, dinner. I reminded Rita of our short meeting at an LSU dance so many years before, but, somehow I got the impression she did not remember me, for she hesitated to acknowledge the meeting. Before long my brother and his wife had other plans, so Rita and I were left alone. It was love at first sight for me when I received my first kiss from her. After dinner, I borrowed my mom's car and took Rita to her rooming house in Lafayette.

After leaving her boyfriend a few weeks later, Rita and I dated regularly for almost a year while I attended college. She lived only blocks from downtown Lafayette, where she worked as a secretary for an insurance company. It was near the college and only three blocks from my home. Mom let me use her car, provided I was careful driving it. Later, when she learned how serious I was with Rita, she made me promise to finish college before thinking of marriage. Rita had the same provisions but was more direct when she stated one day, "I will not consider marrying you until you finish school and have a job!"

As a senior, I was recommended by the dean of the College of Engineering for a part-time job surveying with a contractor who was constructing a new building on campus. My youngest brother, Bill, who had been in the Air Force and also married to a local girl, was in college with me. Each afternoon at about quitting time, Bill and his wife, Ann, who worked in a lawyer's office, picked up Rita at her office, drove to the campus and then picked me up for a short ride before dinner.

Rita and I dated almost every night. I did my studying in the afternoons when I didn't have to work. This continued until I finished college in January 1947. Several months prior to finishing college, I asked for and received the blessing of Rita's parents for her hand in marriage. On our next date I proposed to Rita. I asked her to look in the car's glove compartment. When she did, she found her engagement ring, and quickly accepted my proposal. She was as excited as I was!

CHAPTER IV

LIFE AFTER COLLEGE IN NEW IBERIA

After the fall semester when I completed my degree, I received an interview for a job. Interviews, I quickly learned, were not plentiful in Southwest Louisiana after WW II. I accepted the only proposal made to me by United Gas Corporation, which was located in New Iberia, Louisiana, a short twenty miles from Lafayette. They were expanding their division office and needed an engineer. Because other offers were not available, I accepted the tidy sum of two hundred dollars per month, or "starvation wages," as I call them now.

With that pittance in hand, Rita agreed to marry me, and on February 4, 1947, we tied the knot in Rayne. It was a hectic two weeks. Graduation, marriage, honeymoon in New Orleans, and then I started work. Two people could not live on my salary, so Rita found work as a cashier at the local electric company shortly after we moved to New Iberia.

At first we rented a room and bath on Saint Peter Street near our offices. We rented from a couple whose husband owned a shoe repair shop. Rita never complained except when exhaustion set in from the long hours of having to stand up at her job. Later the electric company provided chairs for their cashiers, an immediate help and a real job saver for Rita.

Several months later we rented a new three-room unfurnished apartment a block closer to our offices. The unfurnished apartment presented a new problem; we needed furniture! Between our two nearby families, we were able to obtain a bed and a chair. We purchased a table, chairs, and a thirty-inch window fan to keep it cool at night. Air conditioning was out of the question. It was great to leave our previous one-room accommodations, for we had many unused table furnishings, plates, cups, silverware settings, and other kitchen needs for daily housekeeping. It was so nice being able to cook our own meals; Rita's mother had taught her well. Even so, I called my mom on occasion for several of my favorites she made.

The Greyhound bus station across the street from the apartment was a great asset since we were without an automobile. We rode the buses for weekend visits with our parents in Lafayette and Rayne. At times they would drive us back to New Iberia, and other times we rode the bus back.

Rita's father made us a proposition. "If you save five hundred dollars, I will match it with another five hundred dollars so you may purchase a small, new car." It took a year, but we finally saved the money and purchased a new Plymouth for a thousand dollars. It was great—finally we were now free to travel!

A year later, the gas company employed another engineer. He had been an Air Force pilot in Europe and was a new graduate in electrical engineering from the local college. The new man and his wife, Leo and Rexine of Abbeville, were able to rent an apartment above ours, and we became lifelong friends. He worked with me, while Rita and Rexine worked together at the electric company. We had great times together, since all of us were about the same age and enjoyed the same food, drinks, and of course one another's company.

After a few years, Leo could not stand the starvation wages at the gas company, as well as the work, so he applied for re-entry into the Air Force at a major's pay. We kept in touch and visited with them in other parts of the country. Years later, Leo and I again worked together when I was able to employ him in Texas after his second retirement from the Air Force.

Rita and I decided it was time to have children. We were old enough and knew what to do. We tried, but without success. As a last resort, we consulted doctors in New Orleans where we were both tested. Rita had previously had work done on her reproductive organs before we were married that later prevented her from conceiving. The doctors had no idea this procedure would interfere with Rita getting pregnant; my test proved I was capable. We tried all the doctors' recommendations, but nothing happened. After a year or so, I suggested that we adopt a baby. Rita objected, so we remained childless. I do believe that was the only time she objected to anything I suggested! Both my mother and mother-in-law were doubly disappointed.

As a member of the Army Reserve in New Iberia, I obtained my commission as a lieutenant and later was promoted to captain after a several trips to summer camp in Alexandria, Louisiana, and Arkansas, and I also attended a summer camp at the same camp in Wisconsin where I spent some time while in the army during WW II. It was a positive experience, and it helped improve our finances; we were paid a month's Army pay as well as my regular salary from United Gas. During the Korean War, I was fortunate to be on active status in the Reserve and not called to active duty. I was thankful to be able to remain at home and work.

CHAPTER V

LOSSES IN LAKE CHARLES

After four years in New Iberia, doing map drafting, cathodic protection field work, pipeline design and general office work, I was offered an opportunity to gain field operating experience when I transferred to a larger district operation in the Lake Charles district. There I supervised pipeline construction and experienced operating distribution systems in the field. Rita and I discussed the possibilities and both agreed to move. The job was interesting and the experience valuable. We found a nice apartment only a block away from an insurance adjustment agency where Rita once again found a job as secretary. We enjoyed living at that apartment for a year before locating and renting a new three-bedroom home. Once again, additional furniture was required. Rita's mother had no further use for her twin beds, which we accepted. Other small items we needed were then purchased.

In Lake Charles we bought our one and only motor boat where, to my surprise, Rita adapted to fishing. Lake Charles is surrounded by lakes and bayous which provided weekend recreation for us. Rita surprised me with learning to cast using her own fishing rod. She caught her share of fish and enjoyed the outings. Fishing broadened our working life. Golf had not entered our life at this date-- it was too expensive.

Sadness followed us to Lake Charles. First, my father, Howard, age sixty-eight, died on April 23, 1951, in Lafayette of prostate cancer. He had suffered with it for a number of years. Several weeks before his death, his doctors decided to operate even though such an operation was not always advisable in those years. The cancer then spread through his body, and he died shortly thereafter. A few days before he died, he was unable to recognize Rita or me. The cancer had reached his brain. He was buried in Morgan City in my mother's family plot.

Then one Sunday afternoon in June of 1951, Rita's father, William, suffered a heart attack in Lafayette. He had been politicking with his brother, who was a sheriff in nearby Acadia Parish in Crowley. Rather than take him to a hospital in Lafayette, his brother continued on to his home in Rayne. There his local doctor was called and immediately sent him to the nearby Crowley hospital.

Notified of his illness in Lake Charles, Rita and I immediately drove to the hospital. There we met William as well as Rita's mother, Sepha. William was smiling in bed, apparently feeling better after the attack. Because we had not had supper, I asked if anyone wanted to join me for a sandwich. Sepha said she was hungry, so she accompanied me while Rita remained with her father, whom she idolized.

We were gone only a short time. We returned, to find Rita was very upset. Her sixty-year-old dad had died of a second heart attack. Sepha almost fainted when she heard the sad news. Hundreds attended his funeral, for he was such a well-known and well-liked resident of Rayne and surrounding parishes. He, a Protestant, was buried in Crowley in a bi-religious cemetery since Sepha, a Catholic, wanted to be buried adjacent to him when her time came. Sepha was in extreme shock for months after her husband's death. She was a devoted wife for more than thirty-eight years.

Rita's brother, Harold, was in the Army at this time. After his father's death, he soon left the Army and returned to assist his mother in managing the insurance business his father had built from scratch years before. They ran the company for a number of years, but with little success, so they eventually sold it. I sometimes regret that Rita and I had not taken it over and let Harold stay in the Army, which he loved. But if we had followed that course in life, we might not have seen Australia and had an enjoyable lifetime elsewhere—not to mention the many other travels we took.

CHAPTER VI

RETURN TO NEW IBERIA

Three years later I was offered the position of division maintenance engineer in my company's division office back in New Iberia. Rita and I considered the opportunity. Again, she had no objection. Part of our decision was that moving would put us nearer our mothers during their time of bereavement, so I accepted the job and we moved back to the city where our married life had begun.

In New Iberia, we rented a two-bedroom home located just off Main Street on Lewis Street. It was only a short drive to the office on beautiful Main Street, which was lined with age-old live oak trees, and beautiful, Southern antebellum homes. It was also near the city's oldest home, Shadows-on-the-Teche, which was a showplace located on Bayou Teche.

Our new home was of the "Louisiana shotgun type" built in the 1800s—not too wide, but wide enough for rooms side by side. From the entrance door one could see half of the house, all the way to the back screened porch that was adjacent to the kitchen. On the other side were the bedrooms and closets. The backyard was large and private, with bamboo shielding one side and a neighbor's garage on the other. We have great memories of the crawfish boils and barbeques we had in the yard together with old and new friends.

The move provided an increase in income, but with it, I had more travels to make. Now I had the entire division under my jurisdiction, from south Louisiana to Alexandria, west to Lake Charles and east to Bogalusa. I was away from home more but always back for the weekends. Rita kept busy by working at the Texaco Company in the personnel department. It was a change, and it made her happy to be away from her former job as a cashier at the local electric company she had when we started our married life.

In those days we were both mobile. I had a company car, and Rita used the Buick we had bought while living in Lake Charles. Life was great. We enjoyed being nearer our homes again and the rekindled fellowship in New Iberia. I became a member of the Junior Chamber of Commerce and Kiwanis Club because I was too old for the Jaycees.

Around that time I also became a pilot using the remainder of my GI Bill of Rights college fund. After earning my pilot's license, Rita trusted my ability enough to fly with me. The owner of the plane let me use it one weekend. Instead of taking a long flight, Rita and I flew cross-country to Rayne, her hometown, all of thirty miles as the crow flies. The trip from and to home was uneventful. I gave up flying soon after when I discovered that hedge-hopping over trees was a sport! It was, of course, but I also decided it could lead to one's death. I have not piloted an airplane since our days in New Iberia.

A few years later Rita and I bought a home on the east side of town on the St. Martinville highway, not too far from Texaco, where Rita was still working. After purchasing it, we decided we needed even more furniture, and for reasons unknown, we chose to visit New Orleans and the Nu-Idea Furniture store there. We purchased dining room and living room furniture, which remains in use to this day after so many years and so many moves. I also planted pine trees around the northern side of the house that grew to be very tall and stately.

One summer our friends, Ralph and Cassie, invited us to travel with them to western Texas, New Mexico, and Colorado. It was our first long trip, and it introduced us to Texas and Colorado western scenery. It was nice seeing the mountains and breathing the cool, fresh air, visiting Carlsbad Caverns, Colorado Springs, Denver, as well as Loco Hills, Texas.

On weekends I played golf while Rita rested from work, since she had no interest in "pasture pool," as we called the sport. However, she was always ready for dinner at the club. Friday or Saturday nights were club nights. The club was located across Bayou Teche in town, where one could stand on the first tee of the golf course and see the nearby New Iberia post office on Main Street several blocks away. It was across the bayou; we called the club a country club even though it was in the center of town! Now it is a subdivision and the new golf club is a true country club on the north edge of town!

I recall golfing there one windy October day, a stiff northern breeze in my face. From the sky was blowing smoke from a nearby sugar mill. I selected a three iron on our par-three eighth hole, and with great luck the ball I hit ended up in the hole for a hole in one! It was my first, and what a great thrill! Thank heavens it had happened in the evening, for the feat was written up in the local newspaper. Otherwise, because I was a junior employee at United Gas, I probably would have had to answer as to how my accomplishment had occurred during working hours.

CHAPTER VII

A New Venture in Jacksonville

After I'd spent more than ten years with United Gas, a friend, Jack, sales manager of Rockwell Manufacturing Company, offered me a job as sales engineer in Jacksonville, Florida. Rockwell sold natural gas meters, regulators, and valves. I had known Jack through associations at United and annual gas association meetings Rita and I had attended in Chicago, Atlanta, and Texas. He was seeking a sales engineer for Florida since a natural gas pipeline company had plans to bring natural gas from Texas into the state. He thought I could help secure sales of their equipment.

Once again, Rita had no objections for a move, leaving the decision up to me. That settled it—with the prospect of a few more dollars in the paycheck, we moved to Jacksonville during the summer of 1957. Jack, Rita, and I were all happy about the move. Rita and I found an apartment in Jacksonville, and Rita gladly retired from work. It was decided that we could finally live on my salary.

I spent the first month in Atlanta learning the business. The job entailed my being away from home, sometimes, for a week at a time, traveling in the northern half of Florida in order to acquaint local manufactured and liquefied petroleum companies of the advantages of natural gas coming to the state. Rita put up with this valiantly. In fact, her only requirement of me in our time in Jacksonville was that

I attend a dance class each Friday night. Usually after being on the road for a week, away from home, one might not care too much for attending a class for a month or two, to learn to do the cha-cha. But I did! How could I not agree with my lover!? Regardless, I don't believe, after learning the dance step, we used it at many dances thereafter.

After six months in Jacksonville, we purchased a new home. It was just off the Beach Highway in Love Grove Acres, only six miles from the Atlantic Ocean and Jacksonville Beach. I joined the Ponta Vedra golf club adjacent to the Atlantic Ocean. Rita, an avid swimmer, enjoyed swimming at the club while I played golf with neighbors and prospective customers. She enjoyed Jacksonville and made friends in our small subdivision.

My job entailed calling on and entertaining prospective customers which included having dinner parties, luncheons, and providing tickets for sporting events and other good will activities. One event that Rita and I were very happy about was obtaining tickets to the world-renowned Masters Golf Tournament in nearby Augusta, Georgia. We attended several tournaments and renewed the tickets for a number of years even after we moved away. That was a terrible mistake; I should have continued my annual membership. I could have sold them or given them away to others who were anxious to attend. Later, when I tried to get back on the list, I realized my mistake; the list was closed because of the popularity of the event. Now tickets are selling on the black market for thousands of dollars.

Jacksonville also offered many other notable sporting events, such as the Gator Bowl and University of Florida football games against the University of Georgia. We enjoyed many of those games with customers. It was also the home of a large engineering firm, Reynolds, Smith & Hills Consulting Engineers, an old and respected Florida firm. They had solicited more than forty Florida cities and towns that were interested in constructing natural gas distribution systems once gas became available. They were one of my most promising clients since they had prepared preliminary natural gas designs for these forty communities. I had hoped to convince them to purchase specified Rockwell meters, valves and regulators when distribution plans were completed.

In 1959 I was approached by my friend Harold who worked at RS&H. After learning of my ten years of natural gas design experience, he asked if I was interested in becoming manager of their natural gas department. Their only experienced engineer had left their employment. Once again, Rita and I had to make a decision, for the opportunities for advancement were great.

I decided that sales in the natural gas industry was not as appealing as field design and operations, and with the new job, I would not have to travel as much and I would be at home more, which Rita liked. My greatest problem was resigning from Rockwell and letting them down. After discussing the possibilities with my friend Jack, we agreed that I could better assist them in the new job by specifying their products rather than others on the market. And so I took Harold up on his offer, but my friendship with Jack was not impaired; today we still remain in daily contact via the Internet.

I set up the Gas Engineering Department at RS&H, prepared and reviewed distribution systems designs, wrote a deposition for the feasibility of natural gas for Florida, and appeared before the Federal Power Commission in Washington DC. I was on the witness stand for three days at the hearing in support of the pipeline's application to bring natural gas into Florida. With our help, the pipeline permit was granted.

Only after beginning work with RS&H did I learn that not all of the forty cities the company represented were under contract with them to design natural gas systems. In fact, we were only able to make final designs and supervise the construction of gas systems for Fort Pierce, Leesburg, a portion of Miami, the conversion of Ocala from manufactured gas to natural gas, Blountstown, and several other small jobs. Though there was work for me to do, it seemed the project would not be nearly as large as I had originally thought.

CHAPTER VIII

A CALL FROM WISCONSIN

In January 1961 I received a telephone call from Harrison, a friend I had worked with at United Gas in New Iberia. He advised that he was now working for an engineering firm from Tulsa, Oklahoma. He was calling from the job in Wisconsin where he was managing the installation of new natural gas distribution systems in northern Wisconsin for Milwaukee Gas Light Company. He had been offered the job of division manager there but was not interested. He asked if I had an interest. I told him yes, for it was a most fortunate call for me, since our company, RS&H had just completed all of the Florida gas work and there weren't many future prospects.

Shortly thereafter, Vice President Dean of Milwaukee Gas Light Company in Milwaukee, Wisconsin, called me and asked that Rita and I fly to up there as soon as possible for an interview. It was the middle of January on a weekend when Rita and I landed in snowbound Milwaukee. Dean asked that we stay at his home for the night prior to the interview the next day.

That night, I learned that a southerner from Florida, who sometimes slept with open windows in the winter, should never sleep with the window open at any time during the winter months in Wisconsin; it was zero degrees outside. For the next thirteen years winters that we spent in Wisconsin, I never opened a window!

The next morning, we drove to the company's headquarters in Milwaukee, where I met other officers in the company. I learned that they were expanding natural gas service into cities and towns in the northwest, southwest, and the northeast communities of Wisconsin. Only Milwaukee had recently received natural gas service for their customers. The new area would be known as the Wisconsin Gas Company, a subsidiary of Milwaukee Gas Light Company, and would be composed of two separate divisions.

The company was seeking an experienced western division manger, the job my friend Harrison had turned down. They had already hired an eastern division manager. I was offered the job, which required organizing a staff of engineers and service personnel and included training and supervising mangers in the cities of district offices located in Wisconsin Rapids, Marshfield, Rice Lake, Tomah, Sparta, and other small towns. The job was just what I had been training for all my working years. Rita agreed with this assessment and with the idea of moving, so I accepted the job.

We returned to Jacksonville, and I had no trouble advising RS&H Engineering that I was leaving for greener pastures since there appeared to be little gas work left for us in Florida. They wanted me to remain with them, for they had other plans for me. Regardless, later that month, Rita and I packed our bags and left warm Florida for cold, cold Wisconsin.

We arrived in Wisconsin Rapids, a small town of about fifteen thousand so named because of a dam just south of the city on the Wisconsin River where rapids did appear as the water left the dam. The city was the home of the Wisconsin Consolidated Paper Mill and just ten miles south, in the small community of Port Edwards, was the Nekoosa Edwards Paper Mill, named for the two nearby adjacent communities. The area was also home for the cranberry industry as well as certain American Indian tribes of the past. A local propane gas company had been purchased by Wisconsin Gas and two sons of the previous owner. One of the sons proved helpful to me in finding a place to live as well as office space across the river from his office.

We located an apartment in Port Edwards, just down the river from Wisconsin Rapids, a block from NEPCO, as the local paper mill was named. Just down the street lived the mill vice president and his wife, with whom we became friends. Rita's charm and Southern hospitality had much to do with the acquaintance. She also was helpful to me in establishing an organization as well as providing friendship with others in the area.

I offered jobs to members of the Tulsa engineering firm who had supervised the installation of the natural gas distribution systems for Wisconsin Gas Company. Some were eager to work in Wisconsin while others were not. I managed to assemble a group who envisioned the opportunities in the Wisconsin area. As time went by some were either terminated or left of their own accord. In a short period of time, my division office was active and provided the necessary supervision to maintain the western division.

As a manager of a new company in town, I was invited to join the Rotary Club. This membership enabled me to meet the townspeople, and they were able to meet me, the new general manager. The association was mutual, for Wisconsinites, I found, were just as friendly as our south Louisiana friends. Rita and I loved to socialize and became members of the local golf club, playing golf and having a happy social life. We soon felt right at home with our new acquaintances. Of the friends we made, many remained on our Christmas mailing list for years, and we have visited them during the recent years. Some have also traveled south for a visit with us.

One of my duties at the company was to assist in the acquisition of new customers. The two nearby paper mills were of prime importance since they had been using coal for fuel. Milwaukee sales personnel, with our assistance, made the contacts. We welcomed the many sales personnel who visited us. It took time, but with cooperation from both offices we were able to sell both mills on the advantages and economics of clean-burning natural gas, compared to the coal they were using in the past.

Beside obtaining customers and organizing the districts, another problem presented itself. Milwaukee Gas service personnel in Milwaukee were unionized. Personnel there were attempting to organize Wisconsin Gas, or "the districts," as they were called. Management and I did not believe such an organization was necessary.

I worked with the personnel department in Milwaukee and local personnel who had been contacted about unionizing. I soon learned that the only problem was the difference in salaries being paid to employees of the newly acquired companies. The problem was solved when I was allowed to negotiate the workers' salaries with company management. The Wisconsin Gas Company was not unionized after wages were equalized in all areas.

CHAPTER IX

RELOCATION TO MILWAUKEE

Life in Wisconsin Rapids was exciting after the union problem was solved. Our primary objective was to acquire new customers and maturity in the organization. In October, Rita and I took time to attend the American Gas Association meeting in Dallas, where we were reacquainted with old friends from Louisiana and other parts of the country.

All went well until the latter part of November 1961, when I was called to Milwaukee for discussions concerning a change in management duties. I was to report to the executive vice president, and my former officer contact was to become the company controller. Then in early December, a complete change in organization was proposed. Top managers were being changed in Milwaukee, and alongside this shuffling was a change in the districts' operation. Only one division would operate as Wisconsin Gas Company. Jack C., the division manager of the eastern division, would also take over my area. I was to be the new standards engineer who reported to the legal department. My office was moved to Milwaukee in mid January 1962.

Prior to moving, Rita and I located a lovely two-bedroom apartment in Whitefish Bay, a small community located just north of Milwaukee on Lake Michigan. It was a quaint village located about ten miles from the office, and it was a lovely drive along the lake with little traffic. We also had a built-in exerciser at our new residence. The home was built on three levels, with the bedrooms on the third floor. Our neighbors were most friendly and hospitable. The move from Wisconsin Rapids in late January was uneventful, and I started my new job even as changes were continually being made at top management levels. A new president was announced shortly thereafter.

My new duties included securing additional franchises in northern Wisconsin. I worked with an attorney, a friend of my new boss. We were successful in obtaining several new franchises while our president and executive vice-president were being replaced. Jack was made executive vice- president, and I took his job as general manager of district operations. The area I was now in charge of was the combined operations of my former division and Jack's eastern division, which comprised over fifty cites and towns in upper Wisconsin.

After a year in the apartment, Rita found a lovely French style three-bedroom home that was also in Whitefish Bay, just a block from Lake Michigan. Rita often told the story of the real estate agent who asked her if the home had to be air conditioned, because it was so near Lake Michigan. And because she was a Southerner who was so familiar with warm climates, she insisted, "It must be air conditioned, or I do not care to see it!" Needless to say, we didn't purchase that home.

She soon found a suitable place which we did purchase. Of course it was air conditioned and ideal for entertaining. The air conditioning was used part of the year, since Milwaukee temperatures did reach near eighty degrees during the summer. Rita did not believe in removing the storm windows, winter or summer! Even so, we were always cool in the summer with the air conditioning. Rita and I loved that old house! We didn't even mind that it had two stories and the three bedrooms upstairs. It didn't even matter that it had old leaded windows. The living room was huge, had a fireplace, and was large enough for a game room in the rear. A downstairs den was also convenient, with its adjacent enclosed bar built inside a closet. The kitchen was the only room we modernized, adding new counters and a built-in table. Our only need for the upstairs was for sleeping. The exterior was constructed of limestone to complete its French appearance. Of course, all the heating and cooling equipment including the washing machine and dryer were downstairs in the basement. We loved living in that house. I often thanked Rita for her selecting such a wonderful home.

Our detached garage was located about fifty feet behind our nearest door. In the cold of winter, I could tell the temperature just from walking from the house to my car in the garage—whether it was above or below zero. The cracking of the January snow and ice in Milwaukee was a definite clue to the weather as well as the temperature. Another problem was the length of the driveway, which accumulated much snow in the winter. I quickly learned that local service stations were adept at removing snow with snowplows attached to their trucks. Thank heavens I did not have to shovel the white stuff! The village did plow the streets and the sidewalks. My only chore was to shovel the walk from the front door to the sidewalk, only about twenty feet, to permit mail delivery!

Two of our Milwaukee friends—Ruth, who worked in the office, and her husband Andy—suggested we join North Hills Country Club, located inland about twelve miles west of our home. We did so, and it was a most enjoyable investment. Rita finally learned to play golf, and her playing enabled her to make many friends. Consequently, she was elected president of the Ladies Golf Association. Later she was elected president of the Milwaukee Ladies Golf Association, comprising all Milwaukee golf courses. Everyone adored her. And further, her golf improved rapidly. She even made a hole-in-one, which delighted both of us. I was so proud. Her lowest handicap was eighteen, which is pretty low for a casual lady player.

We soon learned that the Milwaukee area was even friendlier than the Wisconsin Rapids area. The golf club became the center of our entertainment. We took golfing trips, played golf with couples on Sundays, and generally made friends with our new associates. I, too, entered politics at the club and served as president in 1974, just before another opportunity to organize a new natural gas company in Texas was presented to me.

Between work, Rita and I made trips to the American Gas

Association in Canada, Chicago, Minneapolis, Kansas City, and Dallas, to name a few. After work hours, I usually recouped my energy with rounds of golf in outings at the club. During a week's vacation, Rita and I flew to the Bahamas one January with golfers from the Milwaukee Golf Association. Suppliers also invited us to trips to Venezuela, Hawaii, and Spain. The trips were educational, relaxing, and enjoyable. Whirlpool was one host with whom Rita and I formed a close relationship, along with their president of sales and his wife. They were so friendly. And my division of the company was selling Whirlpool heaters, ranges and refrigerators.

In October each year, Rita and I, with three other couples from our club, managed an annual weekend golf tour in Door County in northern Wisconsin. The tree foliage at that time of the year was always most beautiful and at the peak of autumn colors. I must relate, with Rita as my witness, that when we played golf on one of the trips, I somehow lost my wedding ring. I always took my ring off my finger when playing golf, and on this occasion it probably fell out of my golf bag. I looked for it over the entire course but never found it. Rita never suggested that I buy another ring, nor did she ever give me another one as a gift. She knew that I had loved only her since our marriage in 1947. I did not require a ring to prove it.

I visited the upstate districts quite often. There were scheduled meetings to keep all employees up to date, including sales meetings, management meetings, and meetings to address business problems. At times I traveled to the districts primarily by car, but sometimes I went by airplane.

Flying, I found, was not always safe, for I just missed being involved in several accidents. (This reminds me of my flying experience as pilot after WWII when I learned to fly then quit after I became too daring 'tree hopping'. Now I was taking chances again!) A Detroit pipeline company owned Milwaukee Gas Light and also had several airplanes available for our use when not required by their pipeline personnel. Milwaukee also owned a twin engine plane, which we also flew for business. I recall one takeoff with Al, our pilot, in Rice Lake, which was located in northern Wisconsin and had a runway that ended at a lake. The landing strip was a short one. On takeoff, the plane's wheels always very nearly touched the water as we became airborne. One day I do believe we did touch the water! No problem resulted, but the thought made it exciting to say the least.

There was one flight to the districts, I remember, that might have killed three of us. We were returning to Milwaukee from a "turn-on of natural gas" ceremony for a town in western Wisconsin named Richland Center, near Madison. We always had a large ceremony with local officials when natural gas was turned on for the community, and I attended each one. The pilot was Joe, from Detroit. I had flown with him on many occasions and knew that he was an experienced pilot, having served in the Air Corps in the South Pacific during WW II. He had recorded hundreds of hours of flight time.

This fateful day was cloudy with a low ceiling. We were above the clouds and flying on instruments. As we came out of the overcast into Milwaukee, our public relations man, Herb, and I were sitting in the rear seat. No one was in the co-pilot's seat adjacent to Joe. I noticed we were flying over a small, nine-hole golf course adjacent to Lake Michigan. It was the same route I took each day to and from the office by car. I realized that the golf course was not near the airport. As we flew over the course and a nearby water tank, Herb and I looked up front and noticed that Joe's eyes were fixed on the instruments. We were about to fly into Lake Michigan! We both hollered, "Joe, pull her up!"

And with that Joe pulled the plane straight up. At that point I thought we would then stall out and crash into Lake Michigan, but Joe recovered very well, thank goodness, and we landed at Milwaukee International Airport several miles away. Had we both not yelled at him, I shudder to think of the consequences.

By the time we were safely on the ground, we were shaking and glad to be there. Of course we had to write an account of the incident. When an airplane comes out of an overcast sky and in toward a lake, it is hard to determine where the overcast ends and the water begins. It all looks the same! From that day on, whenever the co-pilot's seat was open, I always sat there to assist the pilot—if only while he was on instruments.

Another time we reserved the DC-3 from Detroit to travel to Richland Center, the same little town mentioned above. There they had only a small airport with a hangar located near the end of the runway. A wire fence surrounded the airport. Landing had its moments, but taking off was almost impossible with so short a runway. On this particular day only three or four of us were on board the DC-3. For takeoff, the pilot positioned the airplane's tail almost touching the fence at the opposite end of the hangar. He revved up the engines as high as the brakes would hold the plane on the ground, then he ran down the runway as fast as the motors could move the plane. When I saw the hangar go by, I thought we were going to crash into the fence! Somehow we were airborne; we must have missed the top of the fence by inches. I breathe a sigh of relief, and I thought twice about ever again using such a large plane on such a small runway. Air travel is faster and easier than driving, but I don't believe it is always worth the dangers involved.

Thirteen years had passed since the districts were formed and had developed as designed. I was enjoying life. The Milwaukee personnel were friendly, but office politics were beginning to show their ugly head for the first time since the restructuring in 1962, and that is one game I did not play. My work took most of my day, even some after hours. Every day it seemed I was on the telephone for hours with the seven district managers I had in the area. I believed, too, that changes were about to be made in the company's near future.

CHAPTER X

FIASCO AT THE WOODLANDS

I recall that while attending a meeting in Chicago in October 1974, I ran into Ben, a vice president of United Gas I had known so many years ago in New Iberia. He then lived in Houston. I mentioned to him that after thirteen years in the Midwest, I was about ready to move back down south. He mentioned that there was a new city under construction near Houston, The Woodlands. It was located just north of Houston, near Conroe, and was being developed by a large Houston natural gas drilling company. I thought nothing of this at the time and enjoyed the convention.

Then Ben called one day the following May, and advised me that he had been offered the job at The Woodlands, but he was too old for it and was ready to retire from United Gas. He asked, "Are you interested?" Before I could answer, he went on to explain, "The job requires organizing and managing a new natural gas distribution company for the new city."

I thought what a fine way for me to end my career and be nearer home. So, with no objection from my agreeable Rita, a few days later, I flew to Houston for an interview with the president of the company that was developing the city. The interview focused on my ability to design and develop a natural gas company I had been involved with during the many years since graduating from college. I would be in total charge as the executive vice president of the Woodlands Gas Company, with an increase in my present salary. It seemed to be my next and final step in attaining the job I sought in my chosen field.

They suggested, and I agreed, that a contract be required. Several days later my lawyer friend and I reviewed the contract that the company submitted, but countered with a few additions and changes. I then discussed the offer with my Milwaukee boss, Jack. He countered with an offer of a raise in salary but provided no advice concerning my worries of a forthcoming change in management taking place at Milwaukee Gas. Hindsight says I should have taken Jack's offer, for there was a clause in the contract with Woodlands that "either party could give the other party thirty days' written notice to terminate the contract." Another stipulation stated that if the gas company was sold, I would be given a position with the parent company. Regardless of the questionable contract concerning the thirty-day provision, Rita and I decided that I would take the job and move south again.

I started work on August 12, 1974, having bought and moved into a lovely two-bedroom house in Conroe, Texas. The Woodlands itself was only in the construction stage. No homes had been offered for sale when we needed one. Our new home, River Plantation, was in a golf course community only a few miles north of The Woodlands. This suited Rita just fine. She started playing golf immediately, and quickly made new friends. After a short while, it was almost like we were still in Milwaukee, only nearer a golf course.

Our new home was vintage 1975, having been built by a couple who was leaving the area. We found it to be a bargain and a good investment. It was one of the latest one level model homes with two large bedrooms, a dining area, a den, and a large living room with a detached garage. I checked its location to ensure it was well above the flood level that this particular subdivision had suffered from in the past, and it was. Rita enjoyed its many features, of which air conditioning was a most important one. Trees were abundant on the lot, but so were the falling leaves in the fall!

The job at The Woodlands was similar to how it was at the beginning at the Wisconsin Rapids job. I started from scratch. A company was already constructing the city streets, including installing electrical, sewage, and water infrastructure. They, however, knew little of natural gas distribution construction. My office was located in a newly constructed building, and I was told by my new boss, "The gas company is all yours."

First I hired a secretary who took excellent dictation. That made organizing the office and the preparation of written procedures easier. My first duty was to change the method that the workers were installing the natural gas mains. The coordinators on site had been installing the gas mains in the same ditch as the water mains, electrical wires, and telephone conduits.

Natural gas mains, they soon learned, were to be installed in separate ditches throughout the development, for the simple reason that natural gas is easily ignited when a leak develops. If all utilities are in the same ditch, and maintenance is necessary, one or all of the utilities can be exposed to damage. Natural gas, if ignited, would cause the most trouble for it could explode if a leak occurs. Therefore water, electric, telephone and other utilities should be in separate ditches for safety purposes. One night there was a fire in one of the ditches that contained electric, telephone and natural gas. It was minor, but could have started a huge fire had if it had not been brought under control within a few minutes.

I also learned that the gas company had not yet received authorization from the state to legally operate. With the help of the legal department, I immediately filed an application with the Texas State Railroad Commission. Operating procedures, drawings of regulator stations, meter installations, and piping requirements—all the plans were quickly made. I represented the gas company in the application process, and with our filed documents, the permit was approved. We were then able to sell natural gas to the few homes already completed on site.

My friend, Ben, in Houston was very helpful. He recommended an accounting associate to set up an accounting system for the new company. I also employed a local retired gas manager to inspect the installation of gas mains. When the gas was turned on, I hired a former Wisconsin Gas service superintendent I knew to be in charge of the service department. Later I hired Leo, my old friend, as my engineer, who had retired from the Air Corps. We had worked together many years ago at United Gas in New Iberia, and it was great being together again after all these years.

The local gas company in Conroe was selling natural gas to us at a commercial rate. Such a price was not suitable for making a profit. The developer I worked for owned more natural gas than we needed. With that in mind, I prepared a study that proved the company could not make a profit buying gas from the local gas company. The developer was interested in the feasibility study and asked me to discuss the situation with an individual I thought was a member of the firm. Later, I realized he was a consultant sent to determine if the Woodlands Gas Company could be a profitable entity. My study was intended only for owner/management reviews in an effort to convince them to sell Woodlands Gas Company gas at wholesale prices, which would enable a profitable situation for the company.

About this time, in 1975, there was a turndown in the economy in the area. Construction of streets and homes in the development was being reduced, and it was questionable if the project could survive. In an effort to cut expenses, a number of the development personnel were laid off. I also learned at this time that the individual I had discussed the gas company with was actually using my study to prove that they should sell the gas company to my old company, United Gas Corporation in Houston. I had been set up by an imposter who was not completely honest with me. Still, I felt secure in my future, for there was a clause in my contract that stated if the gas company failed or was sold, they would employ me in another division of the company.

I had some conversations with my superior, who assured me that though nothing was being done then, if it came to more layoffs, I would be the last one to go. What a deal! I called his attention to my contract and was half-heartedly interviewed by a superintendent of one of the pipelines the company owned in west Texas. Of course, he said I was overqualified and making too much money for his area. The Woodlands Gas Company had obligations to exist since we were already serving customers. I was given several extensions of time on the job. Eventually it was suggested that I discuss my situation with another vice- president of the company who was in a position to offer me severance pay. Before I made any contact with him, I discussed my situation with an attorney, who recommended I consider suing the company. The only problem he believed that may have hurt my case was the agreement I signed, which included the right for either party to terminate our obligations upon thirty days' notice.

Meanwhile, I immediately circulated my résumés to companies throughout the United States. I had a few interviews in Houston, but nothing definite. One consulting firm wanted me to move to New York, which I refused. Finally, on November 30, 1975, I received notice that I had a month's vacation coming to me from Woodlands Gas Company and that after November 30, 1975, I was no longer in their employment. It was the only job from which I was terminated.

I sadly related the information to Leo and the other men I had hired. My secretary left immediately, and Leo ran the company for a few months. It was hard telling Leo, who had moved directly from the Air Force into retirement to be with me. He later found a job with a gas company in Arkansas, and the serviceman I hired from Wisconsin found work with or opened his own air conditioning company in Houston.

Rita and I were devastated with the thought of me having no job after giving up a good one in Wisconsin. I did learn that several months after I left Milwaukee, there was a huge shake-up at my old company. In it my former boss was moved to Detroit, and an individual I was surprised to believe was capable was made president of the company. His buddies were similarly promoted to assist him. Later I learned that sure enough, the new president ran the company into the ground, and the local electric company bought them. So my inclination of a pending change before I moved turned out correct. I understand my old job was given to one of my subordinates, who moved to Wisconsin Rapids to direct district operations from the local office there; that position was a definite downgrade of my former status.

CHAPTER XI

SYDNEY, AUSTRALIA BOUND

I received a long-distance telephone call on November 10, 1975, from Ernie, one of my former bosses in Milwaukee. He had just returned from Australia, where he had been offered a job to provide operating management instruction for an eight-hundred-mile natural gas pipeline then under construction. Williams Brothers of Tulsa was in charge of supervising its installation. They were the same company that designed and supervised construction of the Wisconsin districts for Milwaukee Gas Light—the same districts that I operated.

Ernie was not interested in the Australia job, but Williams Brothers asked about me since they had received my résumé. Ernie said if I was interested, he and his wife, Susie, would fly to Houston the next day and then the two of us would go to Tulsa for an interview. I said, "Come on over!"

They arrived the next day. Ernie and I flew to Tulsa the following day, while Rita entertained Susie at home. We met with George, a vice president who was in charge of the work in Australia. He explained that they were in need of personnel with expertise to activate and train Aussie personnel to operate the new pipeline after the training period. I explained that I was a natural gas distribution engineer and manager, not a pipe liner.

As we discussed it further, I told George that I would consider the job provided they send an experienced pipeline manager or superintendent with me. They informed me that they had a pipeline superintendent who just retired from a large pipeline company who would be perfect as my assistant. The company suggested I fly to Australia, look the job over, and meet with the Pipeline Authority personnel there who would operate the pipeline as an Australian government entity. We settled on a salary, and I agreed to start work with Williams Brothers on December 1, rather than take the long trip to Australia and return to the States for Christmas. The decision to accept the job was made upon Ernie's advice since he had just completed the eighteen hour flight to Australia and another eighteen hour back. He admitted it was too tiring. Williams Brothers suggested I spend Christmas in Australia and take a later vacation there. I agreed

With that settled, I instructed my attorney to bring suit against Woodlands Gas for not adhering to our contract because they had been unable to provide another position for me within their organization. After leaving the country, I found that nothing came of that; the case was never brought to court. As I understand it, there was a two-year filing restriction with which we never complied. Regardless, I felt it might have been a losing proposition. At least I did not miss a payday or an enjoyable experience, which seemed to increase annually. Friends I had made years ago seemed to always appear at the most opportune time with a helpful proposition. I attribute a lot to my devotion to my job, regardless of where it was—and also to a wife who was so adored by all of our associates.

On December 8, 1975, Rita and I packed our bags and flew to Sydney, Australia, via Hawaii, where we spent the night at the Sheraton Waikiki Hotel on Waikiki Beach. The next night we left for Sydney. Rita spent most of her time in bed recuperating from packing and the trip. I decided to go to the beach. There, on the beautiful, white sandy beach, I reviewed pipeline procedures while others were concerned with sunning and swimming. It was an opportune time for me to review my handbooks and pipeline procedures prior to arriving in Sydney on December 10, their time. (A day is lost crossing the International Date Line in the Pacific Ocean.) It was a total of eighteen flying hours from Houston, and it was very exhausting flying in the crowded tourist section of the plane.

Steve, the Williams Brothers manager, met us at the airport. He dropped us off at the Noah's Northside Gardens Hotel located just north of Sydney, where we were happy to relax on dry land and lay in a bed. He suggested we take a boat ride the next day around Sydney Harbor and the surrounding bays. He believed it would improve our health and help the jet lag.

We agreed and took a Sunday boat trip around the bays, where we saw the renowned Sydney Opera House, which was just as beautiful as advertised. Its spread wings are known throughout the world. It was awe inspiring to see, and the vision will live in my memory forever. As predicted, our boat ride around the beautiful bays was also most helpful in curing jet lag. Steve knew what he was talking about.

Our three-room apartment in the hotel was our home for three months. We were located just east of the Sydney Bridge, built years ago. From our balcony, the opera house was in full view, together with the red terra-cotta roofs of the homes, which reminded us so much of San Francisco. To our left, or north, we could see the superhighway extending northeasterly along the Tasmania Sea toward Newcastle, along with the many beaches.

We soon learned, among many other things, that Australia was different from the USA. First, we noted the English custom of driving on the left side of the road was standard. Australia was also a former English penal colony. A great many years ago, criminals from England were sent to Australia and lived in the penal colonies there. Many remained after serving their prison terms, married, had children, and helped populate the country. We also discovered firsthand that the most inhabitable parts of the country are along the coasts. The interior is basically desert, known famously as "the outback," where small, shallow rivers and streams are numerous. Pipeline construction, I learned, had been delayed due to the many abnormal rains.

Australia is about the same size as the United States, excluding Alaska and Hawaii. Its political boundaries include six states, two mainland territories, and several external territories. The majority (75 percent) of the thirteen million–plus inhabitants live in the state capitals. The people of Sydney and Melbourne alone make up over half of the total population. Climate ranges from the tropical and monsoon in the northern regions to the alpine country in the south. The snowfields of the Australian Alps are larger than those in Switzerland. The wide climatic range and the absence of extreme conditions are reasons Australians are great lovers of the outdoors and, as a result, are a highly sport-conscious people.

From North Sydney, I drove the five miles from my apartment to the office in a four-door Ford company car. Driving in Australia was a new experience for me. I was given a company car (with the steering wheel on the right side) one Saturday afternoon. Rita and I took a ride. She read the map, and directed me into downtown Sydney during the rush hour. Knowing how well she could read a map made it easier for me to navigate while on the "wrong" side of the street. But I continued to have to remind myself that the left side of the street was the correct side. We drove through the maze of traffic as if we were old hands at it. We found South Beach Road, which was not as crowded as downtown Sydney. There we stopped and I rested before returning to our hotel.

I soon learned to drive comfortably. Later I passed the driver's test and was granted an Australian driver's license. When I applied, I quickly learned that all measurements, speed and distance, for instance, were in the metric system. With study I was able to pass the test. I did tentatively ask the clerk how many answers I was permitted to miss, and the gentleman replied, "None!"

When I told Rita about the experience, she said, "I will not even try to pass their driver's test!"

I learned later that I could have retained my U.S. license to drive there, since I was working with an Australian permit. Rita did drive a few miles, but I handled most of it during our stay.

Shortly after settling in, I flew the eight-hundred-mile pipeline from Sydney to Moomba, in the state of South Australia, which was the source of the natural gas supply. Flying the route, I did not see any desert. The earlier rains had provided enough moisture for vegetation to grow and cover the outback. It was very lush and green when I saw it.

The flight was uneventful, but my overnight stay was another story. A 266-mile section of the pipeline was under construction by an Italian contractor. American and Australian contractors were installing the other two sections into Sydney. The Italians' camp was complete with a mess hall, temporary sleeping accommodations, construction equipment, and manpower, all from Italy. The workers there, I soon learned, refused to have their pictures taken. The reason was simple. Italian police authorities were looking for men who had committed crimes in Italy and had fled to Australia. I was also told that snakes roamed the desert at night where we were located. The workers suggested I remain indoors after retiring for the night.

After a dinner of Italian goodies, I was assigned an air-conditioned hut for the night. The temporary, mobile-type trailer consisted of a single bed with an air conditioner installed above the foot of the bed. It was working very well in the warm night air when I retired, but about one or two o'clock in the morning, I was awakened by a thumping sound. I assumed the air conditioner had fallen on the bed from its installed location. I quickly discovered, however, that it had not fallen. The motor sounded as if it had exploded, and it was definitely out of commission; not an ounce of cool air could it produce. Sure, the machine was not working, but thank heavens it was still bolted to the wall, at least!

To make a long story short, I remembered ominously the advice the locals had given about the roaming snakes in the desert, so I tried to sleep without any cooling device. Because there was a screened door at the entrance, I was able to open one of the doors for at least some circulation. It helped, but I had trouble sleeping, for the desert was extremely warm that night, and all I could think of were desert snakes just waiting for me to step out of my hut.

The next morning, my next-door neighbor asked, after I told him of my air conditioning problems, "Why didn't you knock on my door? I had two beds; you could have slept in one of them."

When I told him of my fear of snakes in the desert, he laughed even harder. Then I realized I must have fallen for a "snake in the desert" joke. Nevertheless, I was glad to not have taken any chances for snakes are not among my favorite animals. We went together to have an Italian breakfast, which appeared to be a continuation of the same dinner meal served the night before, so I ate very little.

After reviewing the progress of the work, I returned to Sydney without any other mishaps. When Rita saw the condition I was in, she wanted to know what had happened to me. I appeared exhausted, as if I were on my last leg. The lack of sleep, together with having jet lag, did not help. I also felt as if I was now truly initiated into the desert pipeline construction project, with the threat of nighttime desert snakes! Some did say snakes were noted for roaming in the outback. Whether that was true or not, I refused to find out!

In a few weeks my assistant-to-be, Bill Britt, the just retired pipeline superintendent, and his wife Elizabeth arrived from the States. They were from Texas, where Bill had worked for over thirty years as a superintendent with a large pipeline in Nacogdoches. When they arrived, we took them on the same boat ride we had taken around Sydney to help their jet lag. I believed it helped them recover just as we had.

Bill also participated in writing procedures with me. During the weekends, we drove with our wives to nearby vineyards, the beaches along the Tasman Sea in the South Pacific Ocean, and other interesting points such as old Sydney, the opera house, and the park. Orators would take to the many platforms in the parks and preach their gospel to those who would listen. Occasionally we listened, but we avoided getting into controversial subjects that dealt with topics no one had the power to resolve. It reminded me of Sundays in a London park. We listened. Some spoke of American politics, but we would not enter into any discussions with them. The orators only preached topics for the masses. Some interesting points were mentioned, but they were surely not debatable.

We also visited many of the fine restaurants and became familiar with the Australian cuisine. Their seafood was delicious. The preparation of all food was outstanding, having so many different nationalities that had migrated, bringing their foods with them. The Australians were very adept in preparing their native foods. We enjoyed their lamb, barbecues, and the desserts they served with an English flavor. Bill and I also had two outstanding cooks, our wives, who were enjoying not cooking because they were on their vacation for a short while. On occasion we had breakfast and other meals in the hotel dining room. Breakfast, we noted, was just like being at home. They served the cereal in the boxes it came in, large ones and small ones, just as we did at home, in the States. It was one custom we noted with interest.

CHAPTER XII

THE GREAT BARRIER REEF

Before permanently leaving Sydney for the Control Center in Young, located 250 miles to the east, we decided to enjoy a promised holiday. It was in lieu of not returning to the States for Christmas after arriving in Sydney on December 10, so near Christmas. Two eighteen-hour plane trips to and from the States for a Christmas visit would have been too tiring.

We decided to visit the Great Barrier Reef located northeast of Sydney in the state of Queensland and just south of the city of Townsville. The commercial fight from Sydney to Rockhampton was followed by a helicopter ride to South Molle Island near the Hook Island Underwater Observatory. South Molle Island was just south of Cairns and Townsville, and we selected it because it was advertised as having a golf course. We attempted to play golf on their course, but it was evident that it had not been taken care of for a number of weeks. One round was enough! We did enjoy the accommodations; they were not ravenous, but acceptable. The sleeping huts were similar to old drive-in motels built in the United States during the thirties and forties. There was nightly entertainment that we enjoyed, together with several nice Aussie couples we met. The birds, especially the parrots, were most beautiful in their gay colors of red, yellow, blue, white—all colors of the spectrum. It was a relaxing week, and the trip was beautiful.

The Barrier Reef itself was magnificent to see from the observatory. The boat trip out to it was something else. Aussies in swimsuits, male and female, held onto a rope tied behind the boat and water-skied with their bare feet as the boat moved at full throttle. From the observatory, built of glass ten feet below the water line, we saw large, colorful fish swimming over the beautiful coral reefs. From all sides one could view hundreds of colorful fish and the beautiful coral, pearls, sea cucumbers, and various shells used for making buttons, all obtained from the reefs. We learned that the coral had been attacked by crown-of-thorn starfish that had invaded about three hundred miles of the reef. The animal, we learned, feeds on the, tiny, flowerlike coral polyps that build up on the reef. In a single night an adult starfish can ruin a coral head that may have taken fifty years to grow. The starfish, we learned, were being killed by being injected with a solution of formaldehyde.

An Australian couple we met taught us how to crack and eat coconuts that had washed up on the beach near our cottage. We also visited two other islands while in the area. One part I liked was when a female bartender dressed, or partly dressed, served us the best Bloody Marys we'd had, made with good old Louisiana Tabasco sauce—bottled in England, not Louisiana. Nevertheless, the drink and the server were real. Rita, however, had enough with one drink, so we ambled on! The vacation ended with our return to Sydney, and we having acquired another "down under memory." The trip to the reef confirmed that our earlier decision to have Christmas in Australia, rather than returning to the States, was a good one!

CHAPTER XIII

YOUNG, NEW SOUTH WALES

The control center for the eight-hundred-mile, thirty-four-inch pipeline was located in Young, New South Wales, about 250 miles west of Sydney. The Pipeline Authority was created as a statutory body established in 1973 by the Australian government to plan and build a national and integrated network of pipelines in Australia. Their prime objective was to ensure that the "spaghetti bowl" layout of pipelines in the United States was not duplicated in Australia. Their pipeline, as constructed from Moomba to Sydney, became the longest pipeline in the world.

During construction, the Authority's headquarters were in Sydney together with Williams Brothers, my company, who designed and supervised the pipeline's installation. Tom, in charge of the Sydney office of the Pipeline Authority, reported to the director, Jim, located in Canberra, the capital of Australia. Jim reported to the prime minister. Our contacts, therefore, were very close to the top of the Australian government, and decisions were quickly made.

Young, with a population of twelve thousand, was known as the "Cherry Town on the Olympic Way Highway." It was chosen as the pipeline control center because it was only two hundred- fifty miles from Sydney, and the largest city between the 550 miles of "outback" from the source of the natural gas in Moomba. Because of the sheltered nature of the flat terrain Young was, years ago, found to be most suitable for ewes at lambing time. It was also known for its production of cherries, prunes, and strawberries. In Young, there were also a number of recreation clubs, which included a hilltop golf club together with tennis and squash courts, as well as several English bowling clubs. Most clubs had very good, high-quality restaurants.

An office at Cobar, located about three-hundred miles from Young, was also under the supervision of the Young Control Center. Their office consisted of a manager, office personnel, and a maintenance crew responsible for maintaining the first three hundred miles of pipeline beginning at the source of the natural gas supply from the Moomba natural gas field. The Cobar area was strictly "outback." When working on the pipeline, its crews were required to report hourly to headquarters to ensure of their safety. Cobar was an old Australia town known for its copper mining.

While, I, and others were preparing pipeline field operating manuals in Sydney, I made several trips to Young seeking rental properties—one for Bill and his wife, and the other for Rita and me. I was able to find two "flats," or what we know in America as apartments, under construction. One had just been completed, and the other was in the final stages of construction. Bill was the first to move from Sydney on February 26; therefore, he and his wife moved into the completed flat, and Rita and I later moved into the second one. Each was comfortable and well furnished by the Authority. The flats were approximately nine hundred square feet in area. They consisted of three rooms: a bedroom, a combination parlor and dining room, and a kitchen; it also included a bathroom complete with a shower-not spacious, but comfortable.

Our jobs in the control center were to set up operations as a training center. We were to instill our operating experience into the minds of the Aussies now on the job. Bill handled the controls department and I the construction, electrical, and management. My primary job was to train Bob, a young Englishman, for the job of operations manager. He had previously worked for the government, and had applied for the job. He was selected but knew little or nothing of pipeline operations or the properties of natural gas. In addition, I found his management skills and ability questionable- a square peg in a round hole!

Bill and I attempted to train him in his duties as operating manager to include knowledge of pipeline pressure maintenance, electrical controls, personnel management, construction maintenance, controls measurement, and all aspects of operating a natural gas pipeline. He had much to learn in a short period of time. I worked from a desk just outside his office and attempted to keep him abreast of the operations. At times he was interested, but other times he asked to "put it off until tomorrow." I took detailed daily notes of his training progress as well as his attitude, knowledge retention, interest, and so forth. Later my notes came in handy to reaffirm my experience with him.

In spite of the manager's inability to learn quickly, daily operations performed by others were progressing fairly well. Construction and electrical employees learned their jobs and handled them superior to the manager. It was evident the majority of personnel contacted me for instructions rather than their manager. In other words, the personnel had decided I was the manager. Their faith in the appointed one was as questionable as mine.

My Pipeline Authority office contact was Ian in Sydney, with whom I worked very closely. He was an Englishman in charge of operation development in the Young control station. His staff consisted of three engineers: a pipeline engineer, an electrical engineer, and a mechanical engineer. All of them had trained earlier with a pipeline company in England. They were most helpful and assisted in writing the pipeline operating manuals as well as the training of the Young personnel. They understood the operations.

With their assistance, the procedures we jointly prepared included a combination of both operations and maintenance. They proved most helpful to me when putting the pipeline into operation. Ian and Bill were of great assistance in training the regional manager. It was a chore, for he only wanted to do things his way and was learning little of pipeline operations. What complicated matters more was the fact that he did not know or attempt to learn anything about natural gas's characteristics. His attitude was not always the best, nor did he attempt to improve his knowledge. The latter of these later caused his dismissal.

About that time, I was due a month's vacation after being in Australia a whole year—time that virtually flew by. It meant Rita and I were to fly home for Christmas and the holidays. The trainee manager was to be in charge while I was away. I was not alarmed, for I knew he would be carefully observed by Bill and the Sydney personnel during my absence.

CHAPTER XIV

A BREAK FOR CHRISTMAS

Our Christmas trip home for the holidays actually began on December 4, 1976, with a tour of Singapore and Hong Kong. The hotel in Singapore was a luxurious one complete with a nine-hole golf course. The tour of the city was an educational one, for we visited their parks, port, and even the bar where the "Singapore gin fizz" was born.

A three-day layover in Hong Kong enabled more sightseeing in an old city. The nearest we came to China was peering over a fence while on a tour. I recall taking pictures of an elderly Chinese lady who gladly posed for me with my newly purchased camera. I remember eating at the San Francisco Steakhouse restaurant that served thick, American-style steaks, not the skinny, thin Australian steaks we had been eating over the past year. We also Christmas shopped in Hong Kong at bargain prices. Our mothers received watches, while Rita and I each bought tailor-made suits that were available at rock-bottom prices with only two days of fittings.

The trip from Hong Kong to Houston was normal, with few delays. From Houston, however, our small commuter plane to Lafayette was unable to land because of the fog, which socked in the airport. The only recourse was to fly back to Houston, where we spent the night. We called my brother Bill and his wife, Juanita to have dinner together with us. We also invited Leo and Rexine, our old friends from New Iberia. We dined in the same airport hotel where we spent the night. Because of the weather conditions, our airline was paying for our accommodations, so I picked up the check for the group's meal by charging it to our room.

By the time we reached our room, however, the telephone was ringing. It was a call from the restaurant to apprise us that the airline was only paying for two dinners, not six. "I agree with you," I replied, "and I will pay for the other two couples tomorrow before I leave." All was okay after that.

We left the next morning for Lafayette. Because of the weather, our two-hundred-mile trip to Lafayette from Houston had taken longer than it took us to fly from Hong Kong to Houston! We were met at the airport by my brother Jack. Later, Rita's brother picked us up at my mom's, and we spent the night in Rayne with Rita's mother.

Our holiday at home was a most joyous one for us as well as our mothers, who enjoyed having us with them again. It was nice, too, renewing friendships with our Lafayette and Rayne friends. Our Cajun Christmases were as normal as other years. We always said it was of course, number one as a Christian Holiday and number two- more for the children than grown-ups. Rita always enjoyed her holidays and I always marveled at how she approached a beautifully wrapped Christmas present. The paper was torn away, I surmised, the same as when she was the young girl "Teeta". Of course we attended a few parties with our friends where Christmas cookies, cakes and drinks were served. Our acquaintances were interested in our travels and Australia. It was a most enjoyable visit, and I know our mothers enjoyed having us at home again.

After several weeks at home, the trip back overseas was another small vacation to include a stop in San Francisco for sightseeing and relaxation before the long flight back to Australia. In San Francisco, we were glad to have used a travel agency in Sydney that also had provided a copy of our itinerary to the Pipeline Authority in the event they wished to contact us. It so happened one morning that the Authority called me at our hotel in San Francisco requesting that I stop in Sydney to visit their office before retuning to Young. Something had come up that they wanted to discuss with me. Nothing else was said, and of course Rita and I wondered what it was all about. No information had been volunteered during the short conversation.

The call did not hasten our trip back to Australia, however. We had plans to play golf at Pebble Beach on their renowned golf course. We did play the two days we spent at Carmel Beach. First we played Pebble Beach at the rock-bottom price of sixty dollars for the two of us. (The price in 2008 was more like six hundred dollars each!) We shot reasonable scores, and then we played the nearby Spyglass Hill Country Club course the next day before returning to our hotel in San Francisco.

The following day we were to return to Sydney. We speculated along the way, concerned about the reason for the telephone call asking us to stop in Sydney prior to returning to Young. After arriving in Sydney, we checked into our favorite hotel, Noah's Northside Gardens. I met with Tom the next morning. While I was not entirely definite about what the problem was, I was not surprised when I met with Ian and Tom, who said, "Jim, the manager at the center in Young, is not doing his job. We plan to relieve him of his duties, and we want to make you the manager for at least six months until we find a qualified man. Are you interested?"

I said, "Yes, I am, and I will do the best I can for you."

CHAPTER XV

Six More Months in Young

We returned to Young with a plan to spend at least another six months while I managed the operations of the pipeline. The Tulsa office also agreed; and though Rita didn't say yes or no, she had no complaints for continuing our stay there. Her health was fine, and she was lovely as ever!

The job had not changed for me. The Aussie manager was to be "sacked," as the Aussie phrasing goes. I moved into his former office. John, from the States, was my assistant. He replaced Bill, who had decided to return to the States and home. He wanted to retire again. I knew I would miss Bill, but John was a capable replacement.

On Friday, January 14, 1977, four days after I returned from vacation, Ian formally informed Bob, the manager, that he was no longer needed. He was put on leave, and it was suggested I not tell the other personnel of the move until a few days later. Finally, at the appropriate time, I did inform the supervisors of his departure. They were pleased to learn he was leaving; no one approved of his manner of operations because he generally ignored my advice. I had actually taken over as operations manager as soon as I'd returned to Young. Personnel seemed relieved that I was back and in charge. The trainee manager had not been anybody's friend, nor was he admired by any of his subordinates. Sydney management was not positive whether or not the "sacked" manager would sue them as he promised. They were on the lookout in case that might come later.

The following six months went by quickly because of the workload and the many visitors from Sydney. A number of men were interviewed for the manager's job, but few had managerial experience. Finally, near the end of my six-month stay, I suggested they give Frank, the manager of the electrical department, a chance at the job to replace me. I decided he was the best of the managers on site—not too strong, but he had no problems with his personnel. I gave him a few weeks of instruction before leaving for the States. Later, I learned my choice was not satisfactory to management and he, too, was replaced.

Before leaving Young, Rita and I were given a going away party in Cobar. They presented us with two copper goblets as a remembrance of the copper town. The local golf club surprised us with a party, and we were presented with a barometer. We in turn left a silver plate to be presented annually to the best "Mr. and Mrs. Golfer." Each year it was to be awarded to the best golfing couple at the club. And finally, just before we left, the Young control center had a huge dinner party for us at one of the local supper clubs. We were presented a scroll by Ian who read it in part: *Rita and Jim have served their term of bondage with the Pipeline Authority in Her Majesty's colony of Australia and shall be transported back to Her Majesty's former colony called the United States of America.* The scroll was cleverly prepared and now hangs in my living room bar.

The Aussies were both enlightening and enjoyable to work with. We loved them. And in Sydney, before leaving, we were honored again with two dinner parties: one night with Max (the chief engineer of the Pipeline Authority) and Joy, and the following night we had dinner with Steve (manager for Williams Brothers in Sydney) and Elizabeth. We were extremely thankful; it was so nice of our friends and associates to show such gratitude for our stay in Australia. Our time there will be long remembered, and I do believe my work and Rita's personality will be appreciated and remembered by all we met there. It was an enjoyable assignment—the one and one half years we spent "down under!"

CHAPTER XVI

HOME BOUND

We departed Australia for Fiji on July 2, 1977, and had another relaxing trip on the way to our new home in Tulsa, Oklahoma, home of my employer- Williams Brothers. Upon our arrival at the Fijian hotel in Nandi, the Pipeline Authority had sent a Telex to me that read, "We have just discovered that there are one hundred thousand gigajoules of natural gas missing from the pipeline, and you should be prepared to bring it back to the Young Station immediately!" I answered with, "Sorry, but I am taking them home as a souvenir. Not to worry!" This was a prime example of Australian humor.

Our trip, of course, included golf. The Fijian hotel maintained a small, nine-hole course which we played. Later we learned that famous golf course designer Robert Trent Jones had designed a new eighteen-hole course on the other side of the island at Pacific Harbour. We were advised, too, that the roads were too bad for driving. Therefore, we booked passage on a scheduled commuter flight that landed there.

After repacking our going-home bags, we called for a taxi. The taxi arrived on time, and I gave the driver our destination and that we were going via the airport. We loaded our many bags and drove off toward Nandi, the town we had come from the day before. All was going along well, when suddenly, the driver turned off the paved road and onto a gravel road between sugar cane fields. This was not the road we had taken from the airport the previous day. I asked the driver, "Where are you taking us?"

He replied, "To the airport."

It was not the route we had taken the day before, so I leaned over and whispered to Rita, "Now don't get excited, but I believe he is taking us on this lonely road to rob us. Just don't say anything and everything will be okay."

Farther down the road, at a curve, he slowed down and came to a stop by a small wooden shed with a turnstile adjacent to it. I looked to the right, and I saw a small clearing and a hill between two sugar cane fields. About that time a small, single engine plane came in for a landing. I was immediately relieved, and I paid the taxi driver quickly. Later I would learn that only airliners landed in Nandi Airport; this landing strip was only for small, local planes. When we found that we were at the right place after all, I hastily breathe a sigh of relief; so did Rita.

The plane that was landing stopped, and the pilot helped us load our belongings into the rear seat, where Rita sat alone. Had there been any other passengers on board, there would not have been enough room for the humans and the baggage. It was a two-seat single engine plane that sat four people. I sat up front with the pilot and was happy to learn he was an Englishman and not a native Fijian.

We took off, headed for Pacific Harbour. The trip over was uneventful and took less than an hour. The pilot saw my camera and suggested that he would bank the plane in any direction if I wanted to take a picture from my vantage point. I took a few views then decided to just let him fly as smoothly as possible, and I would just view the countryside as we flew over it. No more banking left or right for me.

The golf course was as advertised: excellent! We met and played with a young couple; then we had a pleasant dinner with them. Of course, I related the story of our taxi ride to the airport from the Fijian hotel to anyone who would listen. The bougainvillea and other subtropical flowers there were in full bloom and beautiful. Rita also counted herself "lucky" when she saw and liked a string of beautiful pearls at a local jewelry shop. They soon became another souvenir for her stay in Australia. The following day, we took a bus back to the Nandi Airport, or, "the real airport," as I called it thereafter. No more cane field takeoffs for me. That aviation adventure reminded me of Wisconsin and my flying experiences there.

Our remaining trip to Hawaii and San Francisco was uneventful. We spent the night in San Francisco and began several more days of sightseeing. Instead of flying to our new home in Tulsa, Oklahoma, home of Williams Brothers, we flew to Chicago where I used several more days of my vacation. There we rented a car and headed for Milwaukee with our friends, Peggy and Jim. After four more days of golf, we continued our skipping around the country before returning our car in Chicago. We then flew to Houston to visit Bill and Juanita. The next day Rita and I arrived in Lafayette and started our three-day visits with our mothers in Rayne and Lafayette, respectively. Then it was off to Houston and more golf with Bill and Juanita before flying to Tulsa, our new home. We were both anxious to learn what my stateside job would be. It was a fine vacation for both of us—the flying, the golf, and the visits with loved ones. All of these are memories we shall never forget.

CHAPTER XVII

TEMPORARY HOME IN TULSA

In Tulsa, the change in assignments began. First they promised me a job as manager of the eastern division. Then it was Milan, Italy, and a few days later Tehran, Iran. Rita put her foot down and said, "No more foreign jobs!" And I agreed.

A prospective job came from Mexico. It fell through. I finally reached an agreement that I would remain in Tulsa, so it was okay for us to go ahead and purchase a home. We visited several houses, finally locating a three-bedroom air-conditioned home not far from the office. Next, came the coordination with my brother for shipping our furniture from our home in Conroe, Texas, which he had lived in while Rita and I were in Australia. We concurred on an arrangement date to move then had a moving van load the furniture.

While waiting for our furniture from Texas, Rita and I moved into a small motel, where we remained until September 15, 1977. When our furniture finally arrived, we found some of it had been damaged. It took time, but we were successfully compensated for the damage as listed in our claim.

During this period of uncertainty and settling into another job with Williams, several old acquaintances from Wisconsin visited Williams Brothers as potential engineering clients. Harrison, a friend from New Iberia, came home to Tulsa from a job he had completed in the States. He was an old timer with Williams Brothers having left United for Williams Brothers years ago. He was the one who alerted me to the Wisconsin job years ago. It felt like old home week visiting him and my old cohorts. Meanwhile, at the office, I was kept fairly busy making estimates for potential pipeline jobs after the Mexican job fell through. My status had not changed or had I been given a permanent assignment.

It was great living in the States again. Rita and I were both satisfied. We had visitors in between a trip I made to New York to discuss two pipeline jobs in the Bahamas. Neither job developed. I also turned down supervisor jobs in Indonesia and Iran. Once again Rita had put her foot down—one of the few times she ever did, but I agreed with her wholeheartedly. Later someone must have looked into my résumé or I mentioned that I had had experience as a sales engineer in Florida for I began being assigned new business development jobs; some in the States and others in the Far East.

Regardless, Rita and I joined Tulsa Country Club for golf as recreation for both of us. It was time that Rita got back on the course to make more acquaintances as she always did. Shortly thereafter, I was asked to do a job in Tunisia and/or Kuala Lumpur. Turning them down, I believe management finally got the message: I was not ready to leave the country anytime soon! Notwithstanding, I was being considered for a project management job in South America. Rita and I were both unhappy about the prospects. Nothing had been concrete since returning from Australia. Finally, I was offered the job of business development international in the Far East while living in Tulsa. And perhaps I acted too fast, for I accepted the job on the spur of the moment. It entailed having the Far East as my territory.

My first trip overseas was on March 25, 1978, with three other Tulsa personnel. We left for Bangkok via Chicago, Tokyo, and Hong Kong, but due to heavy snow in Chicago, the flight was diverted to Denver, Spokane, Tokyo, and then Hong Kong. We could not land there because of bad weather, so we spent the night in Manila. The next day, we flew to Hong Kong and finally arrived in Bangkok that afternoon where we were to present a contract the next day for a pipeline job for the government .We soon learned early the next day when we were to present our bid price, that only junior engineers were present,—no managers. It turned out that earlier in the week that our competition's "bag man" must have delivered a bribe in the form of dollars to those deciding who would get the job. The individuals probably accepted both their proposal and the money. Our company had no "bag man" in its employment. It seemed bribery was a way of life in the Far East. No bribe, no job! I should have known then what my future was in the area.

The other three in the party immediately returned to Tulsa. I flew to Kuala Lumpur, Malaysia, to meet with our representative, Pete K who was the son of a prince, and the one who introduced me to potential customers. We lunched at an exclusive English club. Later, for dinner, we met at his parents' home, where I was truly treated royally.

The next day was Saturday, April 1, 1978, and Pete took me to play on his favorite golf course, The Royal Selangor Golf Club (I still have the hat) where we played in the blistering heat. The April fool was the writer—me—who refused to get up earlier, as requested, to avoid the extreme heat. We played the round as if it was raining, under an umbrella, to keep the sun off our fiery skin. I realized then why Pete had wanted me to play earlier. Actually, he was reciprocating to me for the golf outing I gave him at famous Southern Hills in Tulsa when he visited us there.

From Kuala Lumpur I flew on Sunday to Jakarta to meet with Peter DeJong, another of our representatives from the Netherlands who had been with us for years. He had given me explicit details of what taxi company to take from the airport to the Hilton Hotel on Baja Boulevard. I abided by his suggestion and had no problem getting there. I asked him later why I should have taken the cab he recommended. He answered with, "I didn't want you to be robbed of cab fee, and no telling what else!" I learned a year later that the Hilton Hotel where I stayed was later bombed by terrorists, killing several Americans. My luck and good fortune, it seemed, were still with me.

Peter lived in a modern home with an amazing eye catcher: a beautiful huge fish tank sitting on his chimney mantel. The tanked was filled with colorful fish and water plants. Later he and I visited the government's Pertamina Construction office, which was interested in constructing a pipeline. Then we visited the headquarters of an oil company that was considering constructing a coal slurry pipeline in the area.

Pete was so very popular that he insisted I attended two cocktail parties with him. The streets of Jakarta were overflowing with many automobiles, small motor vehicles, and hundreds of bicycles. Built in the order of Russian standards, there were many traffic circles. The circles, it seemed, retarded traffic progress rather than speeding it up.

Following Jakarta, I traveled to Hong Kong, where I checked into the Sheraton Hotel. There I visited an engineering firm that was interested in constructing a coal slurry pipeline from China to Hong Kong. After discussing our expertise, I concluded that the prospect of installation was far in the future.

While in the vicinity, I purchased a new tailored suit for which Hong Kong tailors are known throughout the world. Exhausted, I picked it up on Friday, just before I left for Tulsa. I looked forward to the plane ride. Rita, as always, was waiting for me. She was so nice to come home to. We spent a quiet weekend together, and no golf!

She and I discussed our separate activities while I was away. I told her, "Traveling is okay, but there is no place like home." And jet lag was catching up with me. It took the whole weekend to recoup for work on Monday. Traveling east, I decided, was always more tiring than traveling west to the Far East. It seemed that losing time was more beneficial to my health than gaining time as one does traveling home, or eastward. After a weekend of rest, I was in the office bright and early Monday morning preparing the many reports required after a two-week trip to the Far East.

CHAPTER XVIII

MOM'S DEMISE

On Saturday, April 15, 1978, my brother Jack called from Lafayette to tell me that he had found our eighty-one-year-old mother dead in her bed as he attempted to serve her breakfast. It was an apparent heart attack. Further, he said he would await my arrival in Lafayette before making any funeral arrangements. With that sad news, Rita and I quickly made plane reservations to Lafayette.

After packing our bags, we left for the airport at 10 a.m. in the small car I had just purchased from one of the auto rental agencies in Tulsa. I decided to take it to the airport in lieu of our newer car, which was safely parked at home. All went well until we were about a mile from the airport. The car's motor stopped as we neared a gas station, but we were able to coast into it. The problem was a clogged gas line and carburetor —easily cleaned, but it took time locating the problem. By the time we had it fixed, we had missed our flight.

We returned to our home, where Rita washed a few things before we left Tulsa on a 2 p.m. flight for Lafayette. Jack was waiting for us with Mom's funeral burial policy. My younger brother, Bill, had arrived, so the three of us went to a local funeral home. We selected a casket and made funeral arrangements. I borrowed Jack's car after dinner, and Rita and I spent the night with Rita's mother in Rayne. The next morning, we picked up Jack and spent the day at the funeral home. Between visiting with friends, we also met with Mom's lawyer, who gave us the contents of her will. At the time, it seemed plausible but later we found it proved to be one problem after another.

The following day Bill picked us up in Rayne, and we attended services at the funeral home. Prayers were offered by the American Legion and the Eastern Stars, and finally the funeral proceedings were conducted by two ministers from the Episcopal Church where Mom was a very active member.

Burial took place in Morgan City, Louisiana, Mom's birthplace, about eighty miles southeast of Lafayette. Dad was already buried there along with our young brother, Gene, and Mom's mother and father. Cousins, aunts, and other kin attended the funeral in Morgan City. Both services were well attended, for Mom had many, many friends. She would be missed by all.

My nephew, Bob, and his wife, from New Orleans, brought Rita and me to the New Orleans airport where we had reservations for a flight back to Tulsa. It was a sad two days in Lafayette and even sadder that Mom was no longer with us. She was such a fine mother to all of us. She continues to be missed.

CHAPTER XIX

TULSA ACTIVITIES

Several days after Mom's funeral and Rita and my return to Tulsa, a friend, Buddy, called. He was with Ford, Bacon & Davis, a consulting engineering firm in Monroe, Louisiana. He called to discuss a possible position for me to manage their engineering department. Rita and I agreed to visit with him, and we did so on Friday, May 5, 1978. We drove from Tulsa on a Thursday afternoon and first visited our friends Leo and Rexine for dinner in Texarkana, Arkansas. After dinner, we drove to Shreveport, where we spent the night.

The next morning, we drove to Monroe. I met with Buddy while his wife, Beryl, entertained Rita. We thoroughly discussed the job. The salary he offered was not enough to interest me, however. In further discussions, he thought I could make more on an overtime basis, but I was still not interested. He said that I had been recommended by two of my former Milwaukee bosses, who were now in Detroit with the pipeline affiliate who owned Milwaukee Gas Light. I asked Buddy to consider offering more money and a share of stock in the company. He agreed to consider both and informed me that he would discuss it with Monroe officers and advise if it was possible.

That night Rita and I drove to Conroe, Texas to meet with my brothers, Bill and Jack, who had driven from Lafayette. We stayed overnight, played golf on Saturday, and discussed a few items concerning Jack, who had been living with Mom while not working—or at least not earning enough to live on. After our early morning golf game and discussions, Rita and I drove back to Tulsa.

Buddy called me a few days later and tried to hire me without management insurance and pension benefits. I told him I was not interested. He later called with another proposition, and I finally stated bluntly, "I will stay in Tulsa, but thanks for the interview. Things are looking better here."

He said, "I understand," and I thought that was that.

After a few weeks in the office in Tulsa, Buddy called again and asked if I could visit with him on Friday of that week. He said he had some better news on the job front. On Thursday, May 4, Rita and I visited with him again. He now had a different job for me. After more discussion, I let him know I would think about it. Rita and I returned to Tulsa on Sunday night.

Another week in the office passed, and Buddy called me at home on Saturday with information that he now had a management offer for me. I gave him a salary I wanted. He said he would discuss it with personnel and call me back.

Upon returning to my office in Tulsa, I learned that Ian, my friend from the Pipeline Authority of Australia, would be in Tulsa (on the twenty-fourth.) Meanwhile, office "scuttlebutt" discussions with friends revealed the promise that I had good possibilities with the company and a possible promotion. On Thursday of that week I finally rejected Buddy's latest offer in Monroe, citing that possibilities looked good where I was. He said if I changed my mind to call him.

On May 30, I flew to Guatemala City, Guatemala to discuss with the government the possibility of crossing their country with an oil pipeline from the Pacific Ocean to the Gulf of Mexico. I met with the government's engineer, Renato, who was interested. I also met with Bill W. of United Engineers, who advised that Williams Brothers should handle the design of any pipeline and installation in the country because he was familiar with us and knew people in our organization.

While there I had reservations at the Camino Real Hotel, where I had the pleasure of riding the elevator and speaking with one of

America's TV stars, Art Linkletter and his wife. They were nice and cordial. I also met Colonel Ardon of the United States Consulate.

Rumors at work continued that I would be promoted to head of business development once the present head was transferred. It was another rumor that did not materialize along with the proposed 10 percent wage increase which also turned out to be only a rumor.

Meanwhile, I made several telephone calls to finalize Ian's visit from the Australian Pipeline Authority. Ian was coming to the States to visit with us at Williams Brothers and other United States pipeline companies. I also made contacts for him to visit Great Lakes Gas Transmission in Detroit and El Paso Natural Gas Company in El Paso, Texas.

On Sunday, June 18, 1978, I flew to meet Ian in Detroit prior to his meeting the next day with officers of the company there. I introduced him to friends of mine, Jack and Mike, two vice presidents. Dinner was arranged with them and their wives. After our return to Tulsa, I escorted Ian through the company, the city of Tulsa, and other places until he left for El Paso and then his return to Australia. It was a pleasure to be with him again and learn of the Aussies' present activities and how their pipeline was operating.

The following weekend, Rita and I were very busy with the visit of brother Bill from Houston and our good friends Leo and Rexine from Arkansas, who spent a few days with us. On Saturday, our friends Horace and Etta Mae from Lafayette also arrived. It was a joyous weekend with all our close friends. Bill left Sunday, and the others left later in the week. I know Rita enjoyed the week even though she had much to do with a full house.

On Thursday, July 6, Rita's brother, Harold, called to tell her that their mother was in the hospital with a pain in her side. That Saturday, Rita and I drove to Rayne to see about her. The doctor recommended an operation that would require Rita to remain in Rayne to care for her mother. I flew back to Tulsa and left the car with Rita.

Monday was a routine day at the office. There was some more confusion; a member of the business development department was being transferred, which I thought would result in my big rumored promotion. However, he was replaced by another old-timer. Another rumor gone astray!

Meanwhile in Rayne, Rita was anxious to get her mother's operation over with. This was one of the first times she'd expressed herself that way. It surprised me, but after all, she had just had a rough two weeks with all the visitors we'd hosted. It did not help when I told her I was making plans for a trip to the Far East.

The next night, I called her to check on the operation. "All is okay," she said. "The doctors removed part of her colon and some adhesions. They say she will be all right."

I could tell in Rita's voice that she was relieved. She sounded so much better than the night before. I flew to Lafayette on Friday, June 14. Rita and my brother Jack met me at the airport at 8:15 p.m.—forty-five minutes late, but I was none the worse for wear. We had dinner at Don's Seafood, Rita's favorite restaurant in Lafayette. I flew back to Tulsa on Sunday after spending the weekend with Rita and her mother.

The following week was normal in the office. I called Buddy to check on the Monroe job status as I prepared to fly to the Far East with the new head of business development. A Taiwanese employee who worked in our Tulsa office and professed to know the Taiwan area joined us, claiming he would introduce us to potential customers in Tokyo and Taiwan.

We flew to Tokyo and Hotel Okura. After a night out in the city with a representative of Mitsubishi, we retired to our hotel for rest after the trip. The following day we had been arranged to meet with a Japanese friend of our Tulsa associate at Mitsubishi. After discussions concerning a potential pipeline in their country, we were invited to lunch. They served us a complete meal in the boardroom of Mitsubishi, one of the largest companies in the world. We were impressed. The company was interested in our expertise and the possibility of a natural gas pipeline to be constructed in the area. The luncheon included several officers of the company who later turned the meetings into a social event, even though our discussions revealed that the possibilities of constructing a pipeline in the near future seemed remote.

To enable us to get an early start the next day, we checked out of our Tokyo hotel and boarded a train for the twenty-five-mile trip to the Tokyo airport. We slept in a nearby Narita Hotel so we could leave on an early morning flight to Seoul, Korea. The next morning after breakfast, we boarded a plane, arriving in Seoul at noon. There we visited with Hyundai Motor Company officers to discuss pipelines at a luncheon in one of their factory lunchrooms. We were served a light lunch consisting of a very clear, light soup which, on my first observation, I was not sure whether it was for drinking or for washing our hands in. Luckily I followed our hosts and learned it was, in fact, a soup. It tasted almost like hot water; no vegetables or meat were evident. The main dish was a delicious fish.

From Seoul we flew to Taipei, Taiwan, arriving about 10 p.m. Because we were so late, our hotel reservation had been cancelled. Finally, around midnight, they reassigned us to two small rooms. We learned later that this very hotel was the one Chiang Kai-shek and his wife lived in when he was ousted from China years ago.

Our associate from Taiwan, traveling with us for the sole purpose of introducing us to prospects, said he knew of several engineering firms in Taipei that were interested in our expertise in the design of pipelines. After the first introductions and a meeting with an engineering firm in Taiwan, we decided his contacts were not very fruitful. As a result he was sent back to Tulsa, and another manager and I continue the trip.

With the war on in Vietnam we could not fly directly to Singapore because the route was directly over the battle zone, so we flew back to Hong Kong, where we changed planes and arrived in Singapore at late that night. The next morning we had breakfast with an employee of Drew Chemical to discuss possibilities in the area. The situation was not very promising, so we flew to Jakarta to meet with Pete, our representative there. That night we ate dinner at his home. The following day, we met and lunched with a Williams Brothers crew working on a project there. I knew one of the men, John, who had worked with me in Australia.

Mike, my new travel associate and the new head of business development, left for home from Jakarta. Meanwhile, I flew to Kuala Lumpur and checked into the Hilton Hotel. There I met Pete, the son of a local prince. He introduced me to Shell Oil Company and the local governmental oil company, Petronas who were considering pipelines in the area. Construction and design possibilities, it appeared were not in the near future which made me question Pete if he had any hot prospects in the area. He had none but I realized we had to be able to keep meeting with prospects in the hope we could be of service whenever it was needed.

It was now Thursday, and I was to catch a plane in Tokyo Friday morning for my flight home. From Kuala Lumpur I flew back to Singapore to catch a Philippines Airline plane to Manila. I made the connection easily enough, but this flight was destined for trouble. We took off and climbed to a leveling-off altitude. Now at least several thousand feet in the air, the stewardess had already started serving drinks. Then without any notification, the plane went into a steep dive, and the overhead oxygen life mask dropped into my lap, almost spilling my drink. We were asked to put our masks on because we had lost cabin pressure.

Luckily, nothing more came of it as we landed safely back at the Singapore airport. Shortly thereafter I learned that the plane we were on was a retired one from Delta Airlines. An announcement was made that the problem would be repaired and the flight would continue to Manila within a few hours. With that information I called the local Shangri La Hotel where I had stayed the previous night for a reservation.

I also demanded my luggage be taken off the plane, for I had decided not to continue to fly on that worn-out plane. I was brought to the flight line where the plane was being repaired. When I arrived, I saw my bag fall from the freight compartment and hit one of the workmen. As I claimed the bag, the workman gave me a dirty look.

My only mistake was not making a new plane reservation for the next day while at the airport. I was under the impression that I could make a reservation from the hotel, but as I soon learned, all ticket operations closed after 5 p.m., I worried all night but was successful the next morning in getting an early morning flight to Manila.

It was a mad rush from Manila to Tokyo, for my Tokyo-bound plane was about to leave Manila when I arrived. However, with the help of a jeep driver who drove me across the field to the connecting gate, I made it just in time! The trip was smooth, and I arrived in Tokyo in time to catch my flight home to the States. Someone was already in my seat, but luckily, I was flying first class for a change, and I was able to claim the seat that had been assigned to me. My seat turned out to be next to *Reader's Digest* magazine's Japan representative, who was flying to Hawaii for the boat races. I spent an interesting eight hours talking with him and learned about the area as well as his life.

After a stop in Hawaii, I landed in San Francisco where I spent the night. I called Rita to inform her that I was in the States again. From San Francisco, I flew to Lafayette where Rita met me. She had remained in Rayne caring for her mother after her operation.

We quickly decided to consider moving to Monroe after I discussed with Rita my experiences on this latest trip to the Far East. We spent the weekend in Rayne and then drove back to Tulsa. Rita was so glad to be on her way home after such a long stay in Rayne. I should say, we were both happy to be on the way home. I took Monday off to try to recuperate from my tiring overseas trip; then I called Buddy to ask if the job in Monroe was still open. I had decided: no more overseas trips! After the last flight scare and the length of the trips in general, I had had enough.

Buddy said, "The job is open, and you should meet with me on Saturday morning at the Ramada Inn in Monroe for breakfast."

I said, "Okay. I'll be there."

Meanwhile in the Tulsa office, I met with two barristers (lawyers) from Australia, who came to the States to prepare my testimony to use against the fired control center manager, Bob, whom I had attempted to train while in Young, New South Wales. After being 'sacked' by the Pipeline Authority, he was now suing them. Before I left Australia, I had agreed to testify on their behalf in the event a suit was filed against them. Preparation of my testimony took a few days which was finally acceptable to me after several rewrites.

I also had the occasion to meet with Mike, our new business development head, who informed me that I was to be in charge of new business development in the entire Pacific Ocean area. I nodded my head, not telling him that my days with Williams Brothers were numbered.

That Friday, Rita and I drove to Monroe and spent the night at the Ramada Inn. On Saturday morning I had breakfast with Buddy, as scheduled, and I visited the office for a briefing of my new job. We agreed on a salary, and I received a share of the company's stock. The company also wanted me there as soon as possible. Directly after the meeting, Rita and I looked for housing. We found something suitable but decided to wait until we actually needed it. That night we had dinner with my new boss and his wife, Beryl.

The next day Rita and I left Monroe by way of Texarkana and briefly visited with our old friends, Leo and Rexine, finally arriving in Tulsa exhausted from so much traveling. On Monday I returned to my office and promptly wrote a letter of resignation to Williams Brothers. Everyone I spoke to was sorry I was leaving and continued their sayings, "But you have so much potential for a bigger job here."

What followed was a flurry of activity. On August 15, 1978, I signed a contract with a realtor for the sale of our house in Tulsa. We agreed to an open house on the following Sunday. Buddy called soon after, saying he wanted me in Monroe on September 5 or before. Then, just after signing a written statement for the court case in Australia, Rita and I invited the two lawyers for one of the last dinners we were to host at our home in Tulsa.

A day or so later, the chairman of my outgoing company's board, David Williams, heard of my resignation and called me into his office to discuss the situation. I told him, "Ever since my return from Australia, I have heard of a few positions for me, but none materialized. Further, the business promotion seemed to be my next long-term assignment, but I do not like foreign travel and being away from my wife so much."

He wanted me to reconsider and tried to relate what was in store for me in terms of future jobs. I politely said, "I am sorry, Mr. Williams, but I have committed myself to Ford, Bacon & Davis and can't change now."

He asked, "Why didn't you discuss your unhappiness with me?"

I replied, "I do not go around standard channels. I only spoke to my boss about the situation, and he did nothing."

He closed with, "This should be a lesson to me. I will try to improve communications in the future."

The next day, the president of Williams Brothers called me into his office with the same question: "Why didn't you discuss this with me?"

I related my side of things. "I only follow the chain of command, and apparently my thoughts ended with George, my immediate boss!" The president tried to reiterate what was in store for me in the business development department, but I told him that it was too late.

CHAPTER XX

RETURN TO LOUISIANA

We packed our belongings and left Tulsa on August 28, 1978, for Texarkana, where we spent the night. The next day we arrived at the Ramada Inn in Monroe, a city of over fifty-thousand inhabitants, our new home in north Louisiana which was only two- hundred miles from Rita and my home towns of Rayne and Lafayette. I started work the next day with FB&D. After a month of visiting vacant homes, we located one under construction that we liked. It was a four-bedroom house on Jefferson Davis Drive in a new subdivision not too far from the golf course we later joined.

I reviewed with Buddy the agreement I had with the Australian Pipeline Authority to testify on their behalf if a lawsuit was filed by the dismissed manager from the Young, Australia control center. He was familiar with our previous discussion and agreed to my time off when the hearing was to be held. I also apprised him of testimony I had given to Australian lawyers in Tulsa. I then waited for a call from Australia.

My first trip from the office was to Detroit with Buddy on Delta Airlines to visit an old associate from Wisconsin Gas, Jack, who had been transferred there as a vice president with Michigan Wisconsin Pipeline Company—Ford, Bacon & Davis's largest client. We provided engineering design and inspection for their construction department. Jack had recommended me to FB&D because we had worked together in Wisconsin for over thirteen years. After the meeting, we returned directly to Monroe. Rita thought this was very nice since I was only gone one night!

FB&D owned a hunting and fishing camp on Clear Lake not very far from Natchitoches, Louisiana, southwest of Monroe, where customers were entertained on weekends. I had attended a weekend there when I worked for Wisconsin Gas Company and was familiar with the routine. My first trip as an employee came early on a Friday afternoon. Officials from Louisiana Gas System in nearby Alexandria hunted and fished with us. Rita agreed again, the short trip was more to both of our liking. We both hoped the long, exhausting foreign travels were over!

My new job title was manager of projects. Five engineers and assistants were under my supervision, and they worked on projects throughout the United States. I coordinated engineering work with inspectors from an in-house department. Before long I learned that the engineers were underpaid and helped increase their wages to normal pay for their job requirements. Buddy approved the raises and let it be known that he would keep his finger in all that went on in his and my departments. I soon learned that he gave only partial delegation of authority to his subordinates. This style was somewhat different; I had always respected the chain of command and discussed plans with my immediate superior. It had never been necessary to call it to my attention. The only problems with the job were minor since I felt I did not yet have full authority in the operation of my department. I decided that I should first demonstrate how I operated as well as how I would always keep him advised of what is going on in my area. The delegation of full authority was not given to me, but later I realize this was Buddy's mode of operation. I had limited delegation of authority. It was a different a management style that I was not accustomed to, and in retrospect, I believe it caused me to accept a move I normally would not have accepted had I decided to operate and ignored this method of operation.

The next problem Rita and I typically faced after moving was having our damaged furniture replaced or repaired. This move was an exception, with only minor damage. Our largest problem instead was with the builder. It was still going to be a few months before he finished the construction. It took so long that I threatened to sue him, but he finally completed all the little things with this comment: "I don't believe I will ever sell another house to an engineer. They are too particular!"

After the fact, I found the man to be sincere and honest. We soon became friends, since he lived only a few houses from us in the same neighborhood.

My work in Monroe was more satisfying than the Tulsa job because I was at home more often. Engineering firms are at the mercy of the public. They must seek jobs generally in places away from home. FB&D sought most of their clients in the United States. I continued to travel but, thank goodness, the majority of work was in the country.

Monroe was the original home of Delta Airlines, which became larger in Atlanta, but they never forgot their birthplace. We had regular flights into and out of Monroe to all parts of the world. It was easy to travel to and from our new hometown with little delay. My company also owned a jet, which, at times, was available for the many trips I made in the United States. Occasionally I hitched a ride on the plane to a nearby airport where I could either visit a client or fly on a commercial flight to my final destination. The best part about most trips being in the States was it permitted weekends at home!

The nearby golf course, Bayou Desiard Country Club, was a blessing for Rita and me. We lived only a few miles away. Rita was able to continue her golf games with a new set of girls with whom she became friendly. In turn, I was able to meet their husbands for weekend play. Sundays were also couples days with our new friends. We found Louisiana golfers just as friendly as those we'd met in Florida, Wisconsin, Texas, Australia, and Tulsa. On Saturdays, I played with my male friends. Food at the club was excellent; therefore, it became our social headquarters.

Golf was Rita's primary exercise besides being an excellent cook and housekeeper. Being alone did not seem to bother her or affect her mood. As a result she did not dislike short trips of mind but it was evident that she was not happy about my trips to the Far East when I was gone for weeks at a time. I wasn't happy with them either. She was an avid reader of books and belonged to several book clubs for years long past. Entertaining was another of her likes combined with dining out, which we always seemed to find the best food in the area. Traveling to exciting places was also one of her likes, and we made a number of trips when I worked in the natural gas industry. She did not like to shop as some women do, but she did enjoy visiting shops where bargains were galore. And I can see her now after returning from a bargain shop with a hand full of bargains! In Monroe, I asked her to purchase a new washer and dryer. She did and as usual she always bought the 'top of the line' which I am now using. They bring back so many memories!

A most important criterion with Ford, Bacon & Davis and other consulting firms was the acquisition of clients. Our livelihood was based upon work we generated. FB&D, I believe, was not the most liberal company for spending funds to attract clients. At least, my department was somewhat frugal. We were reminded to be more conservative when expense accounts were turned in. Perhaps more consideration should have been given to the circumstances rather than the cost of each trip. For instance, New York was bound to be more expensive than Dallas or other such places.

Meanwhile, I was having a few medical problems. Doctors suspected a growth in my left breast. An operation was recommended, and I had it performed at the Saint Francis Hospital in Monroe. All reports were negative; there was no sign of cancer—a welcome relief!

Clients kept us busy at work. On one occasion, I flew to Atlanta to discuss a potential aqueduct for water from Miami to Key West, Florida. After the Atlanta discussions, I flew to Key West to discuss the possibilities with the client. Meeting with them, I quickly learned that we were too late for the design stage, and therefore, we were not able to bid on the project.

This was one reason why companies should always make repeated cold call contacts with potential customers. One never knows when a potential job is in the planning stages. Contacts and more contacts usually generate more business. As a result of FB&D's occasional slowness to make contacts, it was evident that the number of jobs under contract in 1978 was decreasing.

Rita and I spent Christmas in Rayne with Rita's mother. 1979 began with a duck hunt at the camp of Paul Crain, a former client, located at Johnson's Bayou near the Gulf of Mexico in Cameron Parish, deep into southern Louisiana. Don, a cohort of mine, and I met with Buddy, our president Fred, and Miles, our business development manager, for a two-day duck hunt with a lavish meal each day. We killed our share of ducks before the weekend and were well fed during the hunt.

After Christmas and the New Year, I flew in the company plane to El Paso, Texas, to present a bid to El Paso Natural Gas Pipeline for a pipeline they were to construct. Rita came with us, since she and I were to be dropped off in Houston after the meeting to participate in the Interpipe 1979 convention. Rita remained at the airport while we visited El Paso Natural, and several hours later we picked her up and flew to Houston. On the plane, she opened a new cookbook for me to see. It was one with Mexican special recipes. She said, "Surely you didn't know this, but I did not have a Mexican food book of recipes before now. And you know everyone must have one, regardless of the many other cookbooks I already have at home!"

It was true; her kitchen bookcase was already filled with cookbooks from all over the world, but she decided she needed one more. With that in mind, I said, "I think we need one since we don't already have one with Mexican foods. It was a good buy on your part." She smiled lovingly at my comment.

CHAPTER XXI

BROTHER JACK'S ILLNESS

As we were moving about the states, my brother Jack was having a hard time with his life for many reasons—Mom's death, a divorce, and to make matters worse, he had cancer of the throat from his excessive drinking and smoking. His wayward son, John D., who was running around Lafayette acting as a wild man, did not help at all. I had talked with Jack about going into the Veterans Hospital in nearby Alexandria for an examination. I thought they would also "dry him out," as the saying goes. He had already stopped smoking.

On January 4, 1980, the day before his entry into the Veterans Hospital in Alexandria, I received a call at the office from my mother's attorney in Lafayette. He called to tell me that Jack was threatening suicide. I asked that he please meet with him and inform him that I was on my way from Monroe and would be in Lafayette within two hours. I hurriedly called Rita so she'd be ready to leave immediately with me. I picked her up and broke all speed records in driving the two hundred miles to Lafayette.

I found Jack at home with his attorney and a shotgun in the room. I asked Jack what the problem was. He named many, including money, his divorce, his health, and the carrying on of his son, John D. The attorney left us alone, and Jack agreed that he should go to the Veterans Hospital in Alexandria for treatment. Though he agreed, he insisted that we take his new car to Monroe with us. He feared that otherwise, his son would take it and leave the state for heaven knows where. He also wanted his son evicted from the house, to eliminate a primary problem.

With that request I quickly gathered John D's clothes, put them in a garbage bag, and left them at the back door with a note saying he had lost all rights to live with his father and should seek another place to live. The note also said that he should contact me for more information, for I was taking his father to the Veterans Hospital.

Before leaving the house, I noticed a note on the table near the couch where someone had been sitting. My name and my brother Bill's were on the note along with some fractions, which may have been the division of property Mom allocated to her three sons as described in her will. Jack was the majority benefactor. Why I did not take the note with me, I do not know. It had been Bill's belief that Jack had advised Mom's lawyer on how to write the will that Mom eventually signed. I always maintained that Mom, in her kindheartedness and judgment, desired to leave more of her property to the son who needed it most, Jack. I objected to Bill's request for a petition to contest her will, and he never filed one. I thought it best to leave all as it was. Neither of us needed the extra dollars included in the will. I truly believed it was Mom's request as written.

Jack and I left for Alexandria in our car, and Rita followed in Jack's car. We checked Jack into the Veterans Hospital and then drove home to Monroe. Several weeks later, Jack called and told us that the doctors had found cancer and wanted to operate. He pleaded, "Please come and get me and take me from this place. The doctors are all foreigners and can hardly speak English. I don't trust them with such an operation."

I agreed and brought him to our home in Monroe on February 18, 1980, when I suggested he go to MD Anderson Hospital in Houston, the world-renowned cancer hospital. Jack was worried about the cost there and felt his insurance could not handle MD Anderson's costs, so he sought nearby doctors instead. His doctor friends in Lafayette recommended a doctor in Shreveport, only ninety miles from Monroe—much nearer than Houston. But was he skillful enough for the operation?

I went with Jack to Shreveport on his first visit with the doctor to discuss the details of the operation. The doctor informed us that he had been trained at MD Anderson. During his examination and further discussions, I listened attentively as he detailed the operation procedure. As I visualized each move the doctor mentioned, I became very pale and almost fainted thinking of all the flowing blood. The doctor saw me about to pass out and called his nurse to remove me from the room. I later felt better not hearing the gory details of such an operation. Hindsight being perfect, I should have insisted that Jack go to Houston and MD Anderson Hospital. Jack, however, was pleased with the doctor's manner and the details of the operation, so he scheduled the surgery for January 30, 1980.

Rita and I were there for the operation. The tumor and affected glands were removed. After the operation, Jack was placed in ICU, and we returned to Monroe, updated relatives about the results, and hoped for the best. The doctor said it had been a successful operation.

After more hospital visits, primarily by Rita, we brought Jack to Monroe and our home on February 10th, to recuperate until he was strong enough for radiation treatments. Rita was able to take care of him while I was busy at the office. After several weeks, Jack was able to drive to Lafayette to attend to business, including the closing of Mom's will, as he was its executor. During his visits at home he learned of his son's whereabouts. He also was able to have discussions with Mom's attorney and Billy, a banker friend of ours who was accumulating and combining debts of his, his son's, and also Mom's. He returned on March 1st.

Rita managed nursing Jack back to a point where he could take radiation treatments in Shreveport. She was able to handle him with little assistance from me although I was at home each afternoon after work. My brother was a good patient who took his medicines without any objection. I considered the operation a massacre, since his tongue was tied to the bottom of his jaw, and a gaping hole appeared in his throat area. He was not a pleasant sight. One good outcome was that his desire for booze stopped due to the operation and our recommendations. He ate as well as possible and conditioned himself for the upcoming radiation treatments in Shreveport. He even played a few rounds of golf with us. Meanwhile, Rita was her calm self who never complained about the inconveniences. Jack was with us several months while taking radiation treatments. He was well enough to return home to Lafayette on April 10th after the last one.

As events occurred, Jack was only able to benefit from his inheritance for a few years before he died. His divorced wife and his son enjoyed the benefits for several years before she died. Now Jack's inheritance is solely owned by the wayward son, who thankfully has matured and is now an offshore cook on oil and gas drilling platforms. He quickly learned that neither of his uncles would dole out any cash to him the way his deceased grandmother did. I wonder, too, if he realized the education he missed, along with increased income he could have made if he had attended college as his uncles Jim and Bill did. Instead, he followed his father's tracks, a man who dropped out of college years ago after making a few dollars.

CHAPTER XXII

A LEGAL TRIP TO AUSTRALIA

My work at FB&D was progressing, and the engineers were doing their work to my satisfaction. It was becoming routine. Then, on July 5, 1980, I received a letter from Tom, managing director of the Pipeline Authority in Sydney, Australia, saying he wanted to see me to discuss my testimony concerning the pending trial of the former manager, Bob, of the control center in Young, New South Wales. He had been released from his job in 1976, and he was now suing them for damages. Having cleared this possible trip with Ford Bacon, & Davis, there was no problem with my superiors about taking the time off. The trip was a short one, and all my expenses were to be paid by the Pipeline Authority.

I made arrangements to fly to Sydney first class on Qantas Airlines and arrived there on Wednesday, July 16. It was a very pleasant trip over, for Qantas was the elite of all planes flying to Australia. Their service was outstanding—so much better than flying on other airlines in the tourist section, with their small rear seats. One is treated as a king on Qantas.

Arriving in Sydney two days later (one loses a day crossing the date line in the Pacific), I checked into the same hotel in North Sydney, Noah's Northside Gardens, where Rita and I had lived for six months in 1976 while I worked for the Pipeline Authority via

Williams Brothers Engineering. Nothing, I noticed, had changed at the hotel in the ensuing years.

I called Rita to let her know I had landed safely, and then I had dinner with an old acquaintance from Williams Brothers. The following day I flew to Canberra, the capital city, where Tom was located. He told me that we would meet on Sunday with our "barrister," as attorneys are called in Australia. Meanwhile, he wanted me to rest up and be ready for the court sessions. He and his wife then entertained me as royalty, squiring me around the capital, and saw to it that I would not be sorry for making the trip.

With time on my hands, I rented a car in Canberra and drove the two-hour trip to Young to visit with friends, and especially the men I had associated with several years before as a consultant on the pipeline project. Many of the old-timers were still at the center. We had lunch together, and I enjoyed every minute of it. They were a fine group to be with. I also phoned a number of friends to renew old acquaintances. And of course I had to see the golf professional at the Young Golf Club. He was from Lake Charles, Louisiana, and he had proved to be a good friend while Rita and I were there.

When I returned to Canberra, I had more time to myself because Tom had other engagements, but again on Saturday Tom and his wife arranged dinner. Then on Sunday we met with the barrister and reviewed comments in my diary concerning the attitude of the former manager during my attempt to acquaint him with the duties required of him to manage the center. It was clear from my notes that he had his own ideas of how it should have been administered. My and others' experience meant nothing to him. He was going to do it his way in spite of the fact that I had been employed by the Pipeline Authority to do it in a professional way. He had no experience, and I had almost thirty years, but that made no difference to him. There was always "tomorrow!" to get serious with his training.

The hearing began at 9:40 a.m. in the Supreme Court Building in Canberra. I was told I would not be needed the first day because the plaintiff would be on the stand most of that day. I was surprised when I was told I could not hear his testimony.

With another free day at the government's expense, I visited TPA's offices, now located in Canberra, which had been moved from

Sydney. There I met Ian, an old friend from the old days. He and I had discussed many of the problems I'd had with the manager two years ago. Ian then informed me that they were developing their own engineering design team, as most new pipelines do. Consulting engineering is expensive, as they learned from my former company, Williams Brothers.

Back to the business at hand; I learned that the barrister for the defense had the right to possession of my diary prior to my testimony. It was most gratifying that he admitted my notes were well written, and he also mentioned my proficiency at golf, for I had noted in the diary my scores when I played on the weekends. I was happy that I had only played on those days, for it would have been embarrassing to explain any other days; thank heavens, I was always at the office and not cutting out for a round of golf.

The next morning I was scheduled to appear in court at 9:00, and this was the same day I was scheduled to fly home from Sydney at 8:30 p.m. My schedule was so tight that I had arranged, before my court appearance, for a car with a driver to be waiting for me at the conclusion of court, at 4:30 p.m. to take me to the airport. I was on the stand for at least five hours but could not leave until court was adjourned. I was somewhat uneasy testifying against a former associate with his wife in the audience, but I had only the truth to tell. The former employee would have posed a risk if there was ever an emergency because of his limited knowledge of a natural gas pipeline. The risk was too great to take.

I was amused at one of the judge's questions to me near the end of my testimony. He asked, "How would you describe the plaintiff's dress each day at work?"

I said, "Sir, I don't believe he could have passed an army inspection with his dress most of the time."

After completing my testimony, the barrister said of that question, "Jim, you couldn't have answered the judge in a better manner. He had been a judge in the army. That was a masterpiece on your part."

With my piece of the trial over, I flew to Sydney immediately after the end of court and made connections with my 8:30 p.m. flight to San Francisco. Later I learned the former manager did not win his case. He was given two thousand dollars and, I believe, another job with the Commonwealth. It must have cost the government a tidy sum, for it had cost them over fifteen thousand dollars for my testimony. I do believe justice was served in this case, however, and the money spent was worth it.

After landing in San Francisco, I called Rita and Buddy to let them know that I had made the trip home safely and would be in Monroe the next day. Then jet fatigue hit me. I spent the night at a hotel near the airport and arrived in Monroe at 7:40 p.m. the next day, where the love of my life, Rita, was waiting for me at the airport.

CHAPTER XXIII

RETURN TO FORD, BACON & DAVIS

After my return from Australia, it took little time for me to return to my office routine. October was natural gas convention time again. Buddy and I, with our wives, attended the American Natural Gas Association meeting in Vancouver, British Columbia, just north of Seattle, Washington. There we opened a hospitality room and catered to old clients with the hope of meeting new ones. I enjoyed seeing many former associates from other companies I had worked with. The Canadian weather was super and the food delicious. The smoked salmon, I will admit, was my favorite.

Buddy was familiar with the area, having worked there years ago. After the meeting, he suggested we visit Victoria, British Columbia, on the west coast of Vancouver Island, also known as the "City of Flowers." It was on our route to Seattle, where we had reservations to board a plane back to Monroe later in the week. To reach Vancouver Island, we traveled by ferryboat along the river and the Strait of Georgia into Victoria, the capital of British Columbia. Upon arrival we checked into the historic Fairmont Empress Hotel across from the state capitol building. We enjoyed afternoon tea as served in the true English manner.

We spent several days on the island, sightseeing within the city and in the countryside in "a wreck," as the others named the automobile I rented. It did not take long for us to realize why the city was named "City of Flowers." Flowers were growing everywhere. The warm winds from the Pacific Ocean made conditions perfect for a year-round growing season.

We visited Butchart Gardens in a light rain. It is a sunken garden planted within a fifty-five-acre limestone quarry owned by an industrialist, who beautified it beyond description. It was brilliantly and formally landscaped. In fact, Butchart Gardens is known as the Las Vegas of botanical gardens, complete with dancing fountains, vista, and paths that reveal a panorama of color and design. The walkway winded past rhododendrons, ferns, lilies, and primroses of bleeding hearts.

Other gardens there included those of Japanese, Italian, and Mediterranean designs, with showy dahlias and zinnias, seas of roses, hanging baskets, flowering vines, topiary majestic trees, tall foxgloves, and calla lilies so perfect we could not believe they were real. The entire garden appeared more like a gardening catalog than a real-life garden. We enjoyed the sights and were happy to have made the trip. I do not believe we missed anything in our "wreck," which held up and drove so well. It may have been a vintage car, but we had no trouble in it.

On Saturday, we rode a catamaran to Seattle, where we spent the night. I dreaded the thought of riding a boat in open water in an ocean after the seasickness in my army days. The catamaran, however, surprised me. On board I was able to take several pictures, and I actually slept most of the way. It was a smooth ride. After spending the night in Seattle, we flew to Dallas, changed planes, and arrived in Monroe at 9:35 p.m. on Delta Airlines. It was a pleasant week away from home that both Rita and I enjoyed.

Monday was once again a workday. Personnel had a new proposal for us to consider. Did we want to work a four-and-a-half-day work week? Work would begin at 7:30 am each morning, and on Fridays we would only work a half day. The proposal was accepted, and getting up earlier became routine after a few weeks.

A large engineering project came in. It was an invitation to bid on a two hundred thousand–customer natural gas distribution system in Alexandria, Egypt. I was assigned the project and worked on it several days, since it was a rush, rush, rush job—all other trips were cancelled. We forwarded the estimate to the principals over there, but we were sad to learn others had apparently bid the job lower than we had. Another few days of work for naught, but engineering is like that. You win some and lose many.

Ernie, with whom I worked for in Milwaukee, was instrumental in my getting in with Williams Brothers, and the Australian assignment called to give me the scoop on a new pipeline proposed for Bangkok similar to the one I had been involved with on a trip a few years ago with Williams Brothers. I was therefore assigned the job and arranged to fly there at the end of January 1981 to meet with a local engineering firm that was interested in doing the job, but required our expertise in design. I had inherited another rush job!

Even though the Vietnam War was over, it was impossible to fly directly to Bangkok without first going through Hong Kong. I slept there overnight then flew into Bangkok the next day. I met with the local engineering firm whose client planned to construct a pipeline to a new cement plant surrounded by lowlands similar to southern Louisiana's swampy lands along the Gulf of Mexico. The bid was due within a week; making a submission would be practically an impossible feat. I surveyed the job almost overnight, relaying the information via telephone calls to Monroe, since the design and calculations, together with the bid, were to be prepared there. I tried my best to complete the fieldwork with a small map, a camera, and visually. Within a short time I had compiled the information they needed to hurriedly prepare an estimate.

Running, with little time left, I arrived at the airport in Bangkok at 7 a.m. prepared to leave for home on Pan American's early flight. It was late leaving, and we landed two hours late in Los Angles on Sunday morning. From there the nearest I could get to Monroe was Dallas, where I spent the night. I arrived Monday morning at 9 am, meeting Rita.

From the airport I stopped first to drop off the film I had taken in Bangkok for development, and then I rushed home, showered, and was in the office before 10 a.m. We worked on the final estimate and forwarded the bid to our engineering friends in Bangkok.

Just before we forwarded the bid, I speculated that we had little chance of being low bidder when I was told that local, or Far East engineers, were also bidding on the job. Considering our travel expenses for overseas travel and the like, we had little chance of getting the job.

When the Bangkok engineers received the bid, they soon learned we were 30 percent higher than the successful bidder, a company from Singapore. We could not reduce the bid estimate to be competitive, so the job was lost. Had I known in advance that locals were bidding— and I consider Singapore to be local—I would have suggested we not even attempt to obtain the job. Hindsight is always clearer, however. Consulting engineering is like that. Money is sometimes seemingly wasted on travel and estimates made. However, we must travel all over the world in hopes of landing a large job. Advertising our experience with visits to potential clients is a must for increasing the number of jobs. Like I've said before, we win some and lose many!

Rita was one who benefited the most from the trip. My Bangkok engineering friends knew a jeweler who sold me a sapphire ring for her. She certainly deserved a present for taking care of Jack and for tolerating my being away from home again. This was beginning to sound almost like Tulsa. She did enjoy the ring, as it was also our thirty-fourth wedding anniversary. We spent the occasion with Horace and Etta Mae from Lafayette and Leo and Rexine from Arkansas, who visited with us.

I was invited to more hunting and fishing trips at the company camp with local clients. Sometimes I begged off so I could recuperate from my many trips. Next, my brother Jack called to say he was coming for more treatments. This time it was a grafting procedure to remove some of the scar tissue. We said, "Come on over, we have lots of room."

The procedure required two days in the hospital. I was busy, so Rita, once again, made the two-hundred-mile round-trip over to Shreveport to pick him up. He spent two more weeks with us before returning to Lafayette. Rita, the nurse, the taxi driver, and my lover continued to smile through it all.

On March 1, 1981, Rita took a short vacation when she and I flew to Denver for the Midwest Gas Association meeting. The three-day meeting was invigorating, for we saw so many of our Midwestern friends, including many from Milwaukee. While there, we thought we were *in* Milwaukee. Five inches of snow fell. We visited several residential neighborhoods, since my company was considering opening an office there. I was not too interested at the time but was under consideration to be its manager.

Leaving Denver in the snow and returning to Monroe was all I had interest in at the time. With work in the office, I also made business trips to Philadelphia, Dallas, Richmond, and Atlanta. Rita and I also attended the annual Southern Gas Association meeting in Nashville, and then I made other trips to Boston, New York, Valley Forge, Allentown, and Merion, all in Pennsylvania, where we had jobs in progress. As anyone can see, Rita was a valuable asset who helped develop and maintained friendships with old and new clients. Throughout the years her health was outstanding.

After a week of office work, I was asked to fly to Milwaukee to visit my old company, Wisconsin Gas. We heard they were considering a new source of gas supply from Illinois. Rita and I combined a few days of vacation with the business trip. We stayed with a friend and rolled the work in with golf as we renewed friendships with old friends. The short vacation ended on August 10. I then spent a week in Denver calling on potential clients.

When I returned home on the next Friday, I learned that Max, an engineer I had been closely associated with in Australia, was in the States and would visit us in Monroe over the weekend. We met him at the airport on Saturday and proceeded to show him how we lived in the South, including a trip around town. On the following Monday after an overnight visit with us, he was off to Houston for a meeting with a pipeline company there. As they said in Australia, "Do not invite an Australian to visit you in the United States unless you mean it." Max was a true friend. We enjoyed his company and sincerely meant the invitation when we invited him for a visit.

Shortly after his visit I was asked to take charge of the Denver office. I told my superiors, "No, at least not at the same salary. But I would be happy to spend a week or so visiting potential clients."

Sure enough, I was off for another week in Denver. Upon my return, Buddy said, "Jim, you and Rita pack your bags and come with

Beryl and me to New York to attend the American Gas Association annual meeting."

If one liked to travel, I was in the right place! It was almost like Tulsa, but at least I traveled more in the States than overseas. Rita and I enjoyed the convention, which was at the Waldorf Astoria Hotel. We met more of our old friends. Buddy and I also visited a client in Boston one day while we were in the vicinity. After returning for dinner that night, we were able to see a Broadway stage show with our wives.

The year 1982 started badly for me. I argued with Buddy about what personnel should be assigned to a new project that included engineers from my department. Of course, I lost the argument! A few days later, I was asked to ride in the company plane to Denver with our new president and others, including Buddy. At lunch the discussion gravitated to the Denver office and who was to manage it. Several names came up. I was still disappointed with Buddy and the argument I had lost about manpower for a new project, so I blurted out, "I will take the manager's job in Denver!"

Buddy disliked my decision, but the president said, "Jim, it is now yours to run!" While it appeared as a spur of the moment decision, Rita and I had already discussed the job in Denver and actually visited around town checking on available housing to rent or buy when we attended the last Midwestern Gas Association meeting in March of the previous year as mentioned above. Again, Rita said, "If we move, it will be your decision, not mine! You make all the decisions. I understand your concern about how Buddy seldom allows you to run your department as you have had in all your other jobs." So we moved.

My previous discussion with him probably got the best of me. Marketing was happy that I had taken the job, for they had wanted me several months prior, the same as Williams Brothers' late decision! The company agreed to purchase my home in Monroe, alleviating one worry for Rita and me. The next problem was finding a place to live in Denver as well as locating office space in downtown Denver for the branch office.

I learned that X-O Industries, a small company with extra office space, had rented an office in Denver to one of our clients,

Southern Natural Gas Company. We contacted Southern Natural, who introduced us to X-0 Industries, who had a vacant office for rent. We rented it, located in the center of downtown and convenient to many nearby offices. Once we had an office, I hired a part-time secretary who was excellent at taking shorthand, my favorite way to write letters.

"Manager—western division" was my new title together with an increase in pay. The area included the entire western United States as well as the Monroe personnel. I also worked with Ford, Bacon & Davis's office in Salt Lake City, Utah. Their office did not handle pipelines or paper mills, as the Monroe office did. Their expertise was in mining and associated engineering which I discussed with some of my contacts.

Next on the list was seeking a house to live in. After a week of house hunting, Rita and I returned to Monroe on our way to attend another meeting in Houston—the Interpipe Association meeting. We drove to Houston, where we again visited with my brother Bill, who was then President of the Texas Pipeline Company, a subsidiary of Texaco.

After a short visit with Bill, we attended the convention on Tuesday night. It lasted through Thursday, when Buddy joined me to make several Houston business calls. He returned to Monroe, but we stayed away from home until Sunday, after visiting Rita's mother in Rayne over the weekend. Rita was her usual bubbly self; meeting old and new clients while at the meeting, even despite cold she'd caught.

While in Houston, we also visited a hospital to see an old friend, Homer, whom I worked with in New Iberia. We had played golf with him, and he was a best friend. He had been transferred to Houston a few years earlier and was not in the best of health. I was sorry to learn that he died of a heart attack not too long after our visit. I regretted that I was unable to attend his funeral because of my transferring to Denver. I am sure that his family understood my absence at the funeral.

I returned to Monroe with a sick wife. She stayed in bed with that cold for a few days. After her recovery, we left for Denver on March 5, 1982, with the intent of finding a place to live. By the end of the week, we discovered a development of new townhouses near the "tech center" south of downtown Denver and not too far from the office. Located in an attractive area, Stoney Brook was designed with small lovely ponds and lakes surrounding each unit. We were fascinated with the townhouse consisting of two bedrooms and a den, which could be made into a temporary bedroom. There was also a basement that made a good storage area for all our other belongings, including all the junk we had been carrying around for years.

One stumbling block was the cost and a financing charge of eighteen percent. It didn't matter the interest rate; we fell in love with the home and decided to purchase it. On Tuesday, March 9, 1982, after having two of our offerings rejected, our bid of one hundred-eighty-two thousand dollars was finally accepted at eighteen percent interest. As a bonus, the developer gave us 'a small TV set'. What? Such a bargain! At least we received something for the high cost of the purchase price! The development included a homeowners' association which, of course, billed us a monthly fee for maintenance of the grounds. It was our first encounter with a homeowners' association. A fee to mow the small yard was included and very gratifying to me! With a definite home address, I stayed and worked in Denver until March 10th when I flew back to Monroe to prepare for the permanent Denver move.

Even though management had decided I was the man for the Denver job, Buddy was still trying to keep me in Monroe. He remarked that he would not hire a replacement for me, thinking I may be ready to return to Monroe within a year.

Brother Jack was waiting for us when we arrived in Monroe after closing on the townhouse. The next day was Thursday, and I worked in the office. Friday, I was scheduled to be one of the hosts at the company's hunting and fishing camp. It was a "must" date, for the client was Michigan Wisconsin Pipeline, our longtime client for which we provided engineering and construction inspection. After the quail hunt with Jack, I drove my former boss from Milwaukee and three others from the Detroit office to the Natchitoches airport where they boarded their plane for their return home. Then I returned to Monroe to be with Rita and Jack, my brother. The following day, the three of us played golf.

On the Monday following, Rita and I, together along with Buddy's wife drove to Dallas for another Interpipe Association meeting. Buddy met us there. That night we attended a dance sponsored by FB&D and featuring Bob Crosby's orchestra. The next morning after breakfast, we returned to Monroe. It was another hectic time, but with an understanding wife, it was bearable. There was never a dull moment and being married to such a remarkable gal made it all so satisfying!

I was in the Monroe office for the next week, which is when I received my first FB&D company car. Then, on Monday, March 22, 1982, Rita and I started the drive to Denver. It was a long, hard, two-day drive with me nursing a beginning cold. We reached Denver Tuesday and checked into the Granada Royale Hotel which wasn't very far from our new home. I bought Colorado license tags for the new car and shopped for a new refrigerator for the house. The long trip and my cold made Rita sick as well. Our coughing must have sounded terrible to those who heard us, but we made the trip, colds and all, and finalize the purchase of our new home. On Friday, we parked the company car at the Denver airport and flew to Monroe, arriving late that night. Our personal car was waiting for us at the airport. The following week was spent in the Monroe office, where I continued working in two different offices. That week, FB&D conducted an energy conference in Monroe. Friends from Milwaukee—including a new friend, Ernest, the vice president of a local gas company in nearby Alexandria, Louisiana—were in attendance. Ernest was a native of my hometown, Lafayette. When I asked him at the energy meeting if he cared to play a round of golf with me at the local golf course, he was so surprised that FB&D was entertaining on a golf course. Had he been catered to in years past, I believe his relationship with the company would have been much closer, resulting in his giving us much more work. His and my personal relationship continued after his retirement, when we visited one another. Rita and I enjoyed his and his wife's company. There were many enjoyable golf games either at my or his home club. I was so sorry when he died, so young, in his sixties several years later from pneumonia and other ailments.

On Monday, April 5, I flew on the company plane to Dallas

then changed planes to Denver, where I spent the week on company business. Finally, on the Thursday before Easter, I flew to Monroe, where Rita met me. On Good Friday we drove to Rayne to visit Rita's sick mother in the hospital. Rita remained with her mother, and I returned to Monroe. I arranged for one of my former engineers to pick Rita up in Rayne on that following Tuesday and bring her to Monroe. Then, on April 17, Rita and I left on the company plane for Nashville and the Southern Gas Association annual meeting with our president, Buddy and his wife, the Risingers , and Landon, our super sales head. There we saw the Grand Ole Opry and entertained other customers with dinners and play on the golf course. We returned to Monroe on Wednesday, and I worked in the office there for the remainder of the week.

CHAPTER XXIV

LAST COMPANY MOVE TO DENVER

Before finishing packing for our move to Denver, we spent the weekend with Rita's mother in Rayne. Several days later, the van arrived, loaded our furnishings, and arrived in Denver the following Saturday, May 1, 1982. Our weekend was spent unpacking and arranging furniture. Accustomed as we were to moving, we were able to complete the job without too big a rush.

My office in Denver was being organized at the same time as our new home. I continued to make cold calls on prospects as well as visiting existing clients in the area. One complaint I had was the number of telephone calls from Monroe. It seemed I had more conversations with them since moving than I did when my office was there. One change I liked was having more time to think between the many calls.

But my travels did not stop. The week after our furniture arrived, Buddy called asking that I fly to Chicago to attend the American Gas Transmission Conference, which lasted three days. I made several good contacts there and continued blind calls in Denver when I returned. Meanwhile, Rita was making progress in arranging our new home.

Back home in Louisiana, brother Jack was in and out of the hospital taking chemotherapy treatments. He was having problems with the procedure but making the best of it. He was also planning to visit us. We both knew he was downhearted over our move so far away. Monroe was only a two-hour drive from his home. Denver was a flight away.

Rita and I joined Pinehurst Country Club in Denver and played golf together on the weekends. She and I were both too busy to even think of playing during the week. Meanwhile, visitors began to arrive. Brother Bill and his wife came from Houston. He was on a business trip and spent the weekend with us. Then, that Monday, I was off to Reno for the International Right of Way Association meeting, another three days away from home.

Jack's chemotherapy treatments continued. When I was invited to attend a sales meeting in Monroe, I flew to Shreveport on Saturday to see him in the hospital. I visited with him, ran a few errands for him, and spent the night in Shreveport. After lunch Sunday, I drove his car to Monroe prior to the sales meeting scheduled for Monday morning. After the meeting, I met several of my engineers, who told me how things were screwed up and how they were all were hoping for a change. They regretted my move to Denver and resented the existing conditions.

After the meeting in Monroe, I brought Jack's car back to him, visited for a while, and then flew to Dallas for the night. The next day I met with three pipeline companies before returning to Denver.

I continued work in Denver and attended a gas company association meeting with Rita in Vail, not too far from Denver. It was an IPAMS gas meeting of the Mountain Gas Association held each year during the middle of August. When we returned, I received a phone call from Ruth, a friend from Milwaukee who had retired in Arizona, with the question: "Jim, do you know how hot it is here in August?"

"No," I said, and she quickly replied, "It is over a hundred degrees and so hot I can hardly breathe. Can I visit you in Denver to cool off?"

I agreed and met her at the airport a few days later. She spent a week with us absorbing the mile-high cool air. We later found that at times, Denver also was very warm, but it lacked Louisiana's humidity. Ruth's visit was enjoyable, and we all did believe she did actually cool off.

After Ruth left, a week later, the Stovers, Nancy and Gordy, old friends from Milwaukee visited with us. I had just returned from a quick trip to Casper, Wyoming, after meeting with gas companies that were doing very little pipeline construction there. I was announcing that FB&D was now in Denver and ready to assist them when work started again. Gordy and Nancy, a favorite couple we spent much time with while living in Milwaukee, spent a few days with us before visiting their son who also lived in Denver. It was old times again with them. We visited the sights in Denver, Colorado Springs, and the nearby Coors Brewery to taste their beer and compare it to Milwaukee's.

On September 5, Out of nowhere, we received the sad news that my brother Jack had died in his automobile as he was driving to Baton Rouge. It was an apparent heart attack. I do believe his death was caused by his recent chemotherapy, although the coroner decided the heart attack was to be the official, independent cause. Jack had loaded his car in anticipation of taking some food supplies to Laura, his ex-wife, who lived in Baton Rouge. A car traveling in the right lane on Highway I-10 just behind Jack reported that, as they were nearing Port Allen, across the river from Baton Rouge, Jack's car swerved to the left on the four-lane highway and ended up in the left lane ditch. Luckily, the four lanes were separated by trees. The heart attack had apparently caused him to slump over the wheel. The car somehow missed all traffic in the left lane. A lawyer from Lafayette was in the car following him. He stayed with the body until the police arrived and pronounced him dead.

On Monday, Rita and I flew into Lafayette where Jack's son, John D., met us. I helped him with the arrangements at the cemetery. The funeral was the following day. We spent the night with Rita's mother in Rayne. I called Buddy, who wanted to see me in Monroe on Thursday after the funeral. I rented a car, drove to Monroe, met with him and others, then Rita and I flew back to Denver.

I was due in Detroit on Monday for a meeting that the Monroe office had arranged. We were to provide refreshments for an exhibit Michigan Wisconsin Pipeline was having. The gathering included a discussion on next year's contract. Jack, my former boss, had also arranged a golf outing for me with another associate. After some discussion and a game of golf, I flew back to Denver on Wednesday.

It seemed to me someone in Monroe recommended the trip for what turned into a wild goose chase! I did, however, get in a round of golf with Jack, which was worth the trip—although an expensive one for the company. I understand attorneys who were handling our new contract with the pipeline later resolved particulars of our continuing contract with them. My only reason for being there had apparently been for providing a few refreshments and to take in a round of golf with a good friend.

Back at home, we had another visitor time again. My cousin and his wife from Grand Junction, Colorado, were in town for a few days. They visited on Saturday. Then on Sunday, four of our Australian friends from Young arrived. We had, years before, invited them to visit us whenever they came to the States. There's that saying about inviting Aussies rearing its head again! The group included Pat, the town clerk in Young, and his wife Thelma, together with the young couple Mike and Lynn, our former neighbors and the owners of the flat we rented. I played golf with Pat at our golf course, and then we visited Vail, Colorado Springs, Golden, Loveland Pass, and Denver. Rita drove the Aussies around on Monday, since I had to fly to Houston for a sales meeting. After my return, our guests flew to Washington D.C. before returning home. It was nice being with them but so unfortunate that I had had to work while they were visiting. I know they understood.

In between working I was in touch with Jack's son, John D., who suddenly decided to act civil once his father died. Money was on his and his mother's minds. They kept calling me, but I advised them that a banking friend of ours in Lafayette, Billy, was closer to the situation than I. He also knew the debts owed by both my brother Jack and Mom. He was working with Mom's lawyer, who had written her will. It was agreed that all the debts be paid, and if any amount was left over, it would be put in a trust fund for John D., who had no knowledge at all of how to handle money. He was only adept at spending more than he had.

Meanwhile, I received another rush call from Buddy asking me to meet him in Chicago the following Monday. He wanted me there to participate in a sealants presentation to the city of Chicago. The Sealants Company, a division of FB&D, was an old company that had developed a special application to repair old, low-pressure gas mains in cities that were continuing to operate at low gas pressures, either in manufactured or natural gas systems. Buddy had recently become involved in the solvents end of the business because the president had recently resigned. He and the company wanted me to learn how it operated.

I met with him in Chicago on Tuesday, participated in the presentation, then traveled to Madison, Wisconsin, and met with more Sealant representatives, who were introducing the company to Madison Gas and Light. The following day we drove to Minneapolis to see another gas company, and then it was back to Chicago before I returned to Denver on Friday. Another fast and unplanned situation! Rita even mentioned how hard it was for me to make any plans because of the constant interference from Monroe.

I was able to remain in Denver for a few weeks catching up on work before our good friends from Lafayette, Horace and Etta Mae, came for a visit on October 14th. We exposed them to the sights of Denver and shared a cabin with them in nearby Winter Park on the weekend. Snow had already fallen. It was a treat for them, I know, but no one wanted to ski. They left after a few days. We did enjoy their visit even though Rita was busy as usual in the kitchen whenever we did not go out for dinner. As usual, I heard no complaints from her. These were our dear friends who would have—and have— entertained us.

Later in October, Rita and I met Buddy and his wife in Kansas City and attended the American Gas Association Convention. While there, we visited President Truman's library and home. In Kansas City we had our fill of excellent and sumptuous barbeque. After our return to Denver, I flew to Buffalo, New York to discuss a natural gas distribution system for Cavanaugh University. Then I was off to Windsor, Connecticut, to discuss sealants with a prospect. Later I drove to Boston to visit with Algonquin Gas Company, an old customer of ours. I picked up six lobsters and flew back to Denver for dinner with my lawyer friend, Bob, who was visiting from Madison, Wisconsin.

Buddy came to Denver the following Sunday night, and we met Monday with W. R. Grace Company, who was very interested in constructing a water pipeline from the Colorado River to California. It was a one-billion-dollar project that would solve our (or many other companies') monetary problems for years. However, it never got beyond the talking stage.

I spent another week in the Denver office before leaving for pipeline companies in San Antonio, Corpus Christi, and finally El Paso and then returning home. Over Thanksgiving, Rita and I flew to my cousin's home in Grand Junction to be with them. They were surprised that we had flown, but I did not want to take a chance driving four hours over the mountains with the possibility of a snowstorm. It was a pleasant Thursday, Friday, Saturday, and Sunday visit. It turned out to be clear, so there was no reason for us to have flown!

The remainder of the year was spent in the Denver office. Rita and I always managed to spend Christmas in Lafayette and Rayne, and this year was no exception. During Christmas week, we flew to New Orleans, rented a car, and drove to Rayne. On our return trip we visited relatives in New Orleans before arriving back in Denver on the last day of the year amidst a heavy snowstorm. We took a cab from the airport, driving home with snow up to the fenders. As it turned out, 1982 was quite a year—our first in Denver.

Our year-end visit back to Louisiana had recharged me for the next year. Rita's mother was an excellent cook when she was well, but she also had a maid who helped her. Rita's brother Harold and his wife Louise lived next door. Louise was also an excellent cook and loved to entertain. The holidays were always relaxing and enjoyable.

Following our visit with loved ones, my routine was similar to the previous year, but engineering prospects turned out to be not as plentiful as in previous years. New Year budgets seemed to be reduced considerably from 1981. New projects were hard to find. Local companies had reduced their budgets for the year, as well. Since my sales funds were down, my airline expenses were curtailed, even if the majority of them were called by the Monroe folks. The entire 1982 economy was in a slump.

Rita, meanwhile, tried to purchase a set of encyclopedias. She had always wanted a set as a child growing up. She found a way to obtain a complete twenty-nine-volume set from the local grocery store. Each week on Fridays, she religiously purchased a volume until all twenty-nine books were hers. We had the library for them. Looking back on it, I believe I have used them more after all these years then she ever did!

With visits and phone calls from Monroe slowing down, the sales picture looked very bleak, both there and in Denver. Finally, on June 6, 1983, I received a call from Buddy informing me that to reduce expenses, they were closing the office in Denver, and a letter was being mailed to all employees outlining other options. He also said that I would be put on a ninety-day leave. I asked, "Will I be paid during that time?"

He replied, "No, but I expect things to change by then, and we will again open the office."

That night, Fred, the company's former president who had resigned, and the man who had originally approved my hiring, called me from the Denver airport asking me to pick him up. I did so without delay. Over dinner he told me he had come to Denver to discuss FB&D with me. He disclosed that because of poor management ever since he left the company several years prior, the company was now for sale for $27 million. They were speaking to German engineers, seeking a prospective buyer. He asked that I help him secure names of other German engineers. He thought my friend Jack, of Michigan Wisconsin Pipeline, might know some. I called Jack, and he gave me several names, which I gave to Fred. The next day following my conversation with Fred, Buddy called me, asking, "Please let me know of any job opportunities you have with others before you accept them."

He believed he would have another place for me real soon. I said, "Okay, I will," and hung up.

Rita and I discussed the situation, for we had gone through a related situation with Woodlands Gas Company in Houston. She borrowed the next-door neighbor's typewriter, and we started writing my résumé and making a list of potential prospects. We agreed the situation was not too great a hardship for us. My inheritance from my mother was not too large, but with oil royalties, rents, and our savings we were not destitute. I was sixty-one years old and seriously thinking of retirement at age sixty-two, anyway, if nothing was available to my liking and welfare.

After mailing a number of résumés, I spent some quality time on the golf course. I was able to improve my golf handicap with others who also felt the downturn of the economy in Denver. Rita's golf also proved to be competitive. I could not give her a stroke a hole. She was more like a half a stroke per hole behind me. Regardless, we kept playing and simply assumed the future would take care of itself.

For the first time in my working life, I applied for unemployment compensation pay. There were long lines at the office because so many were in my position. I must have looked strange standing in line reading my *Wall Street Journal*.

I discovered that one of the requirements to obtain unemployment benefits was to attend a class in résumé preparation. I learned nothing new, what with the number I had sent out in Houston. Other recommendations included how to present oneself at an interview, and so on. It was a welcomed review. Another requirement was to list, monthly, the number of résumés we sent out. They even asked for the recipient addresses.

I do not know why or how, but we received a local paper from Lafayette discussing the start of a new golf course- community near my hometown of Lafayette located on property south of Broussard on US Highway 90. Rita and I discussed the possibility of moving there since her mother was only thirty miles away in Rayne. After a short discussion with my agreeable wife who loved the game of golf and the proximity of Rayne to LeTriomphe, and her mother, she readily said, "Lets do it." I called the developer to inquire as to the particulars and was informed that they were selling lots while the course was under construction as well as membership in the golf club. I mentioned that I did not want a large lot or one directly on the course, nor did I want one too far from the clubhouse. He answered with, "It's a good thing you do not want one on the course; they have all been sold!"

He then asked, "Who do you know in Lafayette?" I mentioned Herbert, a young man I was in school with. Herbert's father owned the largest clothing and grocery store in Lafayette and was completing the development of the Oil Center.

He replied, "He is the principal investor!" He also asked if I had a friend in Lafayette who could approve the location of the lot. I mentioned my old friend Horace, who later met with him and agreed upon the lot I bought over the phone. It was a small lot located where I could see the clubhouse, and large enough for a three bedroom home, and I would not be bothered with golfers looking for golf balls on my property. It was perfect for our taste! The Denver layoff only hastened Rita's and my desire to retire!!

Back in Denver, a small gas company that was purchasing and selling natural gas called to question my interest in working with them. They liked my background and the contacts I had. After agreeing to a 180-day contract with a salary plus expenses together with a percentage of the gas sold, I was back in business. Somehow, I forgot to advise Buddy of my temporary job!

This job required quite a bit of travel. I was acquainted with a gentleman who introduced me to a Canadian contact who had a supply of Canadian gas. With that information, my new contact and I met the Canadian in Cleveland to discuss the matter. We made a handshake agreement that I would participate in the sale of any gas to an American company I introduced him to. With that, the two of us flew to Detroit and discussed the proposition with an old acquaintance, Michigan Wisconsin Pipeline Company. They suggested we discuss the possibilities with another company in northern Michigan. We did so, and the company showed some interest. I also made contacts in my hometown of Lafayette and flew to Houston for other contacts.

Meanwhile, at home in Rayne, there was another problem with Rita's mother. She was hospitalized in November 1983 in Lafayette with a minor issue. However, the nurses there failed to strap her into bed and, as active as she was, she fell out of bed, breaking her hip. This incident increased Rita and my desire to move back home so we could assist Rita's mother. In fact, that was the straw that broke the camel's back. Rita immediately flew to her mother's bedside and only returned to Denver three weeks later after finding an assisted living home for her mother in nearby Crowley. Rita's brother and his wife turned out to be utterly useless as nurses. Rita had to do it all—

my family, as well as her own! Actually her brother seemed more interested in the Lion's Club than his mother. Similarly, I believe his wife had no desire or was capable to assist Rita's mother, she too was aging rapidly and not in the best of health.

Christmas 1983 found us again in Rayne, both suffering with colds and taking antibiotics. By the end of the year, we returned to Denver via New Orleans with definite plans to sell our townhouse and retire in Louisiana. We soon learned the housing market in Denver was as lousy as business was. Nevertheless, we hired an agent and put our townhouse up for sale.

In the middle of February 1984, Rita flew home to be with her mother again. I had some work in Houston later in the month, so I finished it and then flew to Lafayette on February 24 to spend the weekend in Rayne. Rita, her mother, who was well enough, and the three of us flew back to Denver. We were all glad to be home again, even if this was "home" for just a short while longer. Rita's mother made the trip very well and seemed happy to be with us.

By Easter Sunday, April 22, our townhouse was still on the market. At first, Rita's mother enjoyed being with us. Later, as most elders do, she let us know that she would rather be at her home. Fortunately, our luck was changing. A retiring couple was moving to Denver from Washington DC to be near their son. They offered to lease our townhouse for a year at a very reasonable price. We quickly accepted. It was now time to move.

Ford, Bacon & Davis, however, refused to pay for our move back home. This was the first move I had to pay for out of my pocket! I did decide at that time that I would, in some way, get the money back if ever FB&D wanted me to do another job for them. But as this move was at our expense, we eliminated as much weight as we could. The movers charged by the distance moved as well as the weight of articles moved. I donated my college schoolbooks to the Denver library and gave away other items we did not treasure. Rita believed I could have reduced our hoard even more, but I believed I someday still might have needed some of the "junk" that I planned to move. "To hell with the cost," I said, but she was correct; I did throw away some of the excess goods later!

CHAPTER XXV

Retirement in Rayne

Our retirement destination had always been Louisiana, near Broussard, and this was confirmed when Rita and I purchased a lot in the residential golf community of Le Triomphe. It seemed, though, we had retired six months too early. Only the golf course, some streets, and the clubhouse were under construction. The construction of our home was delayed a few months.

After Rita's father, William's death, the house in Rayne was divided into two apartments. Sepha lived in the front apartment and rented the rear one. To change the floor plan back into its original layout was easily accomplished. The hall wall partition that replaced a door was removed and the door reinstalled. With the conversion, the three-bedroom home then had two kitchens and two full baths. It was large enough to easily store our furniture and boxes in the remaining unused space. This made everyone happy. Sepha too was satisfied to be home again, and Rita and I were happy to have a place to live and store our furniture while our home was under construction. It was a change for us living with kinfolk, but we thought it was more appealing than living in a rental house, a temporary apartment, or a motel for four months.

After moving into the family home, we learned that Rita's brother Harold's wife, Louise, who lived next door, was in terrible condition and was confined to a hospital where she suffered from an incurable disease. We finally understood why she could not help Rita's mother when she became ill. Before we left Denver, we were advised by our doctors to immediately have our medical problems reviewed when we got to Lafayette. My problem came first when my prostate specific antigen (PSA) readings were above normal levels. Rita had begun to complain of having problems finding things in the grocery store that she had been shopping in for almost two years. We feared it might be a memory problem.

My Lafayette doctor monitored my PSA for a few months before recommending that I see an urologist, who reviewed the readings and recommended a biopsy be taken immediately. It proved positive as a malignancy. After a bone and CAT scan he recommended an operation. I suggested a second opinion at MD Anderson Hospital in Houston, and my doctor agreed. He also said he knew a Dr. Von Eschenbach there. I called M D Anderson and made an appointment for November 6, 1984.

A few days later, I met with Dr. Von Eschenbach and Dr. Cohen at M D Anderson. After a thorough examination, it was decided an operation was necessary to examine my lymph nodes and determine if the cancer had spread. The fourteenth of the month was selected, a date that enabled us to return to Rayne for a week, and then drive back to Houston for the operation.

We were thankful when the procedure revealed that there was no indication that cancer had spread into the lymph glands. I was hospitalized for two weeks then spent a night at my brother's home prior to Rita driving me back to our temporary home in Rayne. To support the incision so it wouldn't be damaged, I rode in the back seat of the car holding onto the strap fastened above the door while Rita chauffeured me home during the next three hours.

While we were away from Rayne, arrangements were made for Sepha to temporarily reside in the Rayne Guest Home. She, however, was not happy about the move, but she endured it without too much distress. Like mother, like daughter, Sepha surely was a trooper!

As Christmas neared we were able to write and mail our annual Christmas cards while I regained my strength by walking a few blocks each day and visiting friends in Lafayette. We spent the remainder of the year in Rayne as I recovered and carefully played golf between hospital visits.

Radiation was prescribed for me in Houston, making it necessary that we again find a temporary home for Sepha, who was then ninety-one years young. Since she was not fond of the Rayne Guest Home, we found a suitable place in nearby Carencro, just north of Lafayette and only forty miles from Rayne. We brought her to the temporary home on the thirtieth, and she was to remain there until my treatment in Houston was completed sometime in January.

While under going treatments Harold called to inform us that his wife, Louise, had died. When we asked about the funeral, he said that she had given her body to a clinic in New Orleans for educational use there and that only a memorial service would be said for her in Rayne. He saw no reason for us being there and suggested we remain in Houston to continue my treatments.

Previously I had mentioned Rita's problems to Dr. Von Eschenbach. After my initial operation, Rita had trouble finding my room after going downstairs for lunch. The doctor was concerned and suggested I have her examined in Lafayette before I returned for more radiation. This we did. Our local doctor ordered a CAT scan of her brain, which revealed a growth the size of a potato on the left side of Rita's head.

I immediately called my brother Bill in Houston and asked, "Could we have our room back at your house? We must return to Houston for Rita to visit a neurosurgeon for an opinion concerning a possible operation."

He said, "It's okay with me, but what happened?"

"It is a meningioma, a large growth on the left side of her brain causing her memory problems," I replied. He was concerned about this news, and, of course, gave us full blessing to make use of the room. Then he asked, "How do they remove the growth without harming the brain?"

I replied: "I understand they will use a laser that dissolves it."

" Not to worry, we have lots of room," ended the conversation.

We returned to Houston and saw the doctor, who recommended that Rita be operated on as soon as possible. We drove back to Rayne and returned just a week later for the surgery. It was a long, long, twelve hours waiting for completion of the procedure. The doctor described it to us beforehand; he would use a laser cutting beam to evaporate the growth. I was not alone in the waiting room: a cousin, his wife, and my brother Bill with his wife kept me company during the operation.

Rita came through with flying colors. I visited her after she regained consciousness in the intensive care unit. She was concerned about an argument she had had with the head nurse. Rita, never usually one to complain, told me the nurse had done something she did not agree with. After I calmed her down, she went back to sleep and never again mentioned what the trouble had been. She was in the hospital for two weeks. The doctor also reported that he believed Rita had an enlarged heart, which should be watched. Later, other doctors in Lafayette decided it was not an enlarged heart, but fluid around her heart. An operation for this was performed later.

We thought, with the removal of the meningioma, that Rita's memory would be restored. It was for a while, but in later years her memory became much worse.

We recovered from our ailments in Rayne while planning and designing our new home for construction in Le Triomphe. We attempted to build it around the rooms we liked best in the many homes we had lived in. This took some planning, for we were limited to a home with a minimum of two thousand square feet, without the garage, to be built on a small lot with setback restrictions. I did the rough draft and employed a Lafayette company to complete the construction plans. After the final plans were accepted by the Le Triomphe Homeowners' Association, we sought construction bids from local contractors, a process that took a few months. The lowest bid was given to a contractor who was already constructing homes in the subdivision. Work began in April and was completed in August 1984.

Rita's mother had not been satisfied with her stay in the Carencro retirement home, and although we were not too fond of the Rayne Retirement Home, we finally decided that it would probably be best for her to live there since she had so many friends and relatives in Rayne. Nonetheless, she was not at all happy to leave her home. We hated to move her, but with both of us incapacitated while recuperating, a decision had to be made, good or bad! Rita was gradually becoming more forgetful, which I felt I could handle, but I questioned my ability to handle two people who needed care for very long. I did try for a while, but soon we did, with regret, place Sepha in the Rayne Retirement Home.

Ford, Bacon & Davis called me about that time asking that I do one more job for them. It was a natural gas feasibility survey for a natural gas pipeline just south of Salt Lake City, Utah from Monroe to St. George near the boundary with Nevada. The pipeline's length was about 263 miles, and the distribution systems involved thousands of miles of pipe. I accepted the job with a written contract with the thought of reducing our moving expenses from Denver back to Louisiana.

I was provided two men with limited experience to do the field survey. We headquartered in Salt Lake City and worked on the pipeline route daily, including Saturdays and Sundays. Rita remained in Rayne with her family. After two weeks of field work, I spent a month of weekdays in Monroe designing and writing the report. My weekends were spent in Rayne with Rita. Near the end of the job, I brought her with me to Monroe, where she was able to see old friends while I was working in the office. I completed the job in July but never learned if the project was actually constructed. It didn't matter; I was now completely retired, having collected some of my moving expenses. That was my last job!

During the pipeline job, our home was being constructed at Le Triomphe. I missed the careful inspection I would have given it had I not been in Monroe. As a result, I was only there just before the concrete driveway was to be poured. I learned twenty-four years later that I should have remained a few more hours to supervise the pouring, because now I own a badly cracked driveway. This came even despite my uttering the following parting words when I saw the contractor about to pour the concrete, "Be sure to pull the reinforcements up into the concrete as it is poured."

I said that because the reinforcement steel was on the ground for the length and width of the driveway. It probably still is! Regardless, questionable driveway aside, our new home was completed in August 1984.

Moving from Rayne was another story! We moved on August 19, using a small local moving company from Lafayette. After agreeing to a moving price a week earlier, the owner of the truck, upon arrival in Rayne, claimed the items in the garage had not been mentioned and would cost extra to move. I knew they had been included, for I was there at the time. I told him, "Okay, if I owe you more money, kindly take all the items you just loaded off the truck, and forget about the move today. I will get another mover!"

With that he suddenly remembered that the quoted price included all of the items in the garage. At the same time, he did demand that the move must be paid for in cash, no checks. That, I could not talk him out of, and Rita and I stopped at our bank in Lafayette to cash a check for the full amount of the load! It was the first time I had ever paid cash on the barrel-head, particularly for a local move. Rita and I decided it was to be our last move after so many we had made in the States and abroad.

CHAPTER XXVI

FINAL RETIREMENT AT LE TRIOMPHE

Retirement in Le Triomphe was easy to become accustomed to. At first I played golf four times a week with new friends. Rita was not as fortunate. There were few lady golfers playing in the beginning, but she and I did play together on Sundays when a few other couples played. Rita was so busy arranging and rearranging the house furniture she had little time for golf.

In between golf and seeing friends, we traveled throughout Louisiana and Texas. Entertaining was one of our lifelong habits, and we kept it up. Local friends wanted to see the new house, and we entertained with shrimp, crab, and crawfish boils, always in style in Cajun country. By January 1987, the Le Triomphe Homeowners' Association became active. My comments and complaints were paramount reasons for my election by my friendly neighbors to the board of directors. It was evident to all that many of the published rules of our owner's association were not being followed. I soon discovered that participating in and administrating homeowners' association rules and regulations was very different from governing everyday activities in industry. When working for a living, the rules are more universal and are usually followed without question.

The rules were different in Le Triomphe. For example, even the simple placement of a garbage can in a subdivision governed by a home owners association usually cause questions or complaints. City or municipal rules demands that their cans be used and when and where they should be placed on the street for pickup. A homeowner's association legislates where the garbage cannot be located and that it must be stored out of sight of the neighbors either by being stored in a garage or concealed behind a special fence but never should it be seen by neighbors or from the golf course except on trash pickup days. Any simple rule entails comments from those who don't agree. This example is simple compared to location of fences, swimming pools and other home improvements rules which homeowners expect the alteration of written rules by the home owners association. And in retrospect, I wonder how I endured five years of service, one as president and another year when Rita was very ill with her problem?

On December 23, 1987, the partnership that organized Le Triomphe became a victim of a trusted employee who overspent and missed payment of interest due on their bank notes. The bankers demanded full payment. Since the money was not available, the bank took over ownership and sold the development on September 13, 1990, to Nichiei Louisiana Corporation, a Japanese-owned corporation with offices in New Orleans. They ran it until it was sold again on February 1, 2000 to local investors, Mike and Perry. Mike, the senior partner, later purchased Perry's percentage and now owns the golf course and club in their entirety. He has done an outstanding job in conditioning and beautifying the course. It is now a show place of southwest Louisiana and one of the finest golf courses in the state.

Rita and I were enjoying our retirement and were so happy that we had come back to southern Louisiana. We attended my fiftieth high school reunion in 1988 and quickly noticed how my former schoolmates had matured. I dropped Rita off at the entrance to the reunion, which was held at a nearby country club, then parked the car and walked back to meet her. She said, "Jim, I believe we are in the wrong place. There are too many old people in there."

I replied, "Let's go in and see for ourselves."

Then I mentioned to her that when parking the car, I had almost run over my high school girlfriend, Margaret, whom I had not recognized. All in all, we had a good time reminiscing with the group about our high school lives and the memories the reunion brought back. I learned, too, that Margaret was living in Denver not too far from where we lived for two years. It is still a small world, even though we did not meet her in Denver. It was also apparent that my old classmates were not golfers, for I don't believe I have played golf with any with whom I attended high school. Actually, I believe that now, I may be one of the few still alive.

While I continued to play golf, Rita, with her dwindling memory, was able to drive to and from our home to visit her mother at the retirement home in Rayne. She was careful to take the old route of Highway 90, the highway she was familiar with, and avoid the busy new US Highway I-10 that paralleled it.

In August 1987, my doctor and I agreed it was the necessary time for Rita to visit a neurologist. Her memory was not improving; it was getting worse. We visited Oschner Clinic in New Orleans where she was given an oral memory test to determine her retention criteria. I was in the room with her and found it was extremely hard for me to also remember things on the memory test. Actually, the doctor must have noticed because he suggested I leave them alone. "Why don't you leave the room? Leave us alone, and chew your gum outside," he insisted.

I knew we were both in trouble then.

For a while I thought I may have been the patient because of what I heard and retained during the short time I was with Rita and the doctor. I readily understood why Rita failed the test. My memory was never very good when it came to names. Rita always helped me out. But the doctor judged, from the test, that she had signs of dementia, or the beginning of Alzheimer's! We returned home with the sad news and waited for other medicines from our local doctor.

Shortly thereafter, Bobbie and Cliff, friends of ours from Milwaukee, were going to Palm Springs, California on vacation and asked us to meet them there for a short stay in a home they had rented. We had accumulated a number of airline sky miles from all the traveling we did, so we decided to accept the invitation. We thought it would be okay since Rita was only in the beginning stages of Alzheimer's. We made arrangements to fly to Los Angles, then

Palm Springs for a week of golf and a memorable visit with old friends.

Rita was fine in Palm Springs. We returned to Los Angles, spent a few days sightseeing, then drove to San Diego to visit with Jack, my old retired boss from Milwaukee, and Margaret, his wife. From there we flew to Phoenix to visit Ruth, the girl who had visited us in Denver to "get out of the heat" a year prior. It was another pleasant two weeks, as Rita had no problems with her memory and the new medicine she was taking helped so much. She was like her old self!

We returned home with no other stops, but around that time I learned that my old company, Ford, Bacon & Davis, had sold the pipeline department to a Houston engineering firm. Monroe was now only designing paper mills, and the Salt Lake City office continued in the mining business. Later I heard that another engineering firm I had worked for, Williams Brothers, had also been purchased by another company. Both companies, Wisconsin Gas Company and Milwaukee Gas Light Company, were also sold to a Milwaukee electric company. I had been associated with that gas company for thirteen years. It seemed to me I retired at the right time—while companies I worked for were still in existence. Retirement, I now believe, was worth all the years I spent on the job. And I appreciate what I learned at each one.

More problems arose in May of that year. Rita's mother, Sepha, fell at the retirement home and broke a rib. It seemed that old age catches up to people and businesses. Neither has an unlimited life. I believe there is simply no way of getting out of this life alive, and that goes for companies as well as humans!

In addition to all the grief we had suffered throughout time, we were again saddened with the latest death of Rexine, our old friend from New Iberia. Rita and I attended the funeral and were able to continue life with other friends. In September, we visited Hot Springs Village in Arkansas with Al and Dot whom I met when we retired at LeTriomphe. Al, four years my senior, became my idol for even with a bad heart he has continued life on the golf course. Another LeTriomphe golfer, Jack O. and his wife Jane of Crowley, who owned a home there, along with old friends, Cliff and Bobbie from Milwaukee, had retired in the village after we visited them in

California. The retirement community had many golf courses that we enjoyed playing on. It was tempting to remain there forever, but we quickly remembered Arkansas as having cold winters. Louisiana was cold enough for us. One thing Rita and I knew: no more Wisconsin winters!

In October of 1988, following our trip up "nawth," in Arkansas, Rita's brother Harold, announced that he was to marry his longtime girlfriend, Stella, a former school teacher. His first wife, Louise, had died several years earlier. Rita seemed well aware of what was happening and had an enjoyable time at the reception; a tribute to Aricept, the memory medicine she was taking. Her many cousins were there, none of whom had she forgotten. It was a happy event for everyone; Harold's first marriage had not been as happy as it could have been. This one, we believed, would be better.

Later in the same month Rita and I visited San Antonio where my brother Bill had retired, and invited us to a member-guest golf outing at his club. It was an enjoyable week of golfing and partying. On the last day of competition when we each birdied the number three hole, Bill, my partner in the event said, "Boy, now we have it going; maybe we can win a prize!"

Needless to say, that was our best hole, and we won exactly nothing. We had played as partners a number of times with the same results. Our golfing chemistry must have been bad—at least when we were partners!

Rita enjoyed the event as well, but by the fourth day of a tiring tournament, the night life seemed to have caught up with her. At the closing awards and banquet dinner, she was not able to hold her food. A doctor at our table learned of her relatively recent meningioma operation and decided that probably was the reason. The same night individual pictures were taken of each of the golfing partners and their wives. Our picture appears as though nothing was wrong. She was still her beautiful, smiling self when the photographer said, "Smile!" before snapping the picture. The photo is now prominently displayed on my living room mantel, showing Rita as she really was—always smiling.

Soon after returning to Le Triomphe we learned that Sepha was suffering from stomach problems. A colonostomy was recommended.

We met her at Lourdes Hospital in Lafayette where the procedure was performed. Her prognosis was good, but she was restricted to a diet of soft foods. A feeding tube was also recommended because her esophagus was restricted. This did not prevent Sepha from attending her annual Zaunbracher family reunion and picnic in Roberts Cove, a small German community adjacent to Rayne and the home of her father and mother. She was recognized as the oldest relative of the family at ninety-two years young. She enjoyed the honor.

In December, a tube was inserted into Sepha's stomach for feeding. Soon afterwards pneumonia set in in both lungs brought her to the hospital. We spent time with her until her condition improved and returned to the retirement home. In January, she was again having trouble keeping food in her stomach. I believed it was because she was not receiving the attention required for an older person. With that inkling, I called the state authorities about the poor attention she was receiving. Her care improved somewhat after my complaint, but we saw very little positive results. Anyone at the home was at the mercy of the employees.

In March of 1989, in an effort to relieve the pressure of fluid around her heart, Rita entered the hospital in Lafayette. A short time later, while recovering from her meningioma operation in Houston, the doctors suspected that she had an enlarged heart, but after another examination in Lafayette, fluid was again the culprit which simply required removing the sac around the heart.

Prior to the operation, she took a stress test given by her heart doctor. When I asked how it was afterward, he answered, "Heck, I don't believe she can walk across the street, as bad as the test was!" Spoken like a true doctor who plays golf at LeTriomphe!

Consequently the surgery was postponed until November. By then, her stress test was okay, and the operation was performed. Rita came through very well as expected. She was in the hospital for six days before I brought her home.

About this time, I lost two more friends. A. C. died of cancer, and Billy B., another friend from high school, had a heart attack while on business in Baton Rouge. Billy was the banker who had helped settle my mother's will and clear all of Jack's debts. Both he and A. C. were good friends with whom I had grown up.

After Rita's operation she was placed on stronger medicines to help her memory and depression, which were not getting any better. I continued to play golf as much as I could. I soon found that leaving notes for Rita advising where I was did not always get through to her. And I will admit that I probably forgot to leave a note on a few occasions. Whenever I returned and could not produce a note as evidence, she raised holy hell with me. I tried to do better, for it was not her fault. I had no excuses and understood her position. It was the disease. At that point, I thought a trip might help her.

Our Milwaukee friends, Dr. and Mrs. Klicka, Jerry and Joanie, invited us to visit them in July 1990. Rita agreed to go only if I drove rather than fly. A condition of the trip was that we would drive there in three days rather than to rush and make it there in two. I could not talk her out of it and said, "Okay, three days to drive only one thousand miles!"

Prior to leaving, we visited with Sepha in the retirement home in Rayne to check on her condition. She was under the weather with a bad cold. We discussed it with her caregivers, who thought it would be okay if we took a two-week vacation. And so we began to drive the one- thousand mile- three day trip. We stopped in Memphis on the first day. We had dinner, cocktails, and then we retired for the evening. The next day we stopped in Illinois, and then it was on to Milwaukee where we drove the final 150 miles. It was a long trip; we could have flown there and rented a car for the price we paid for motel accommodations. But Rita wanted it that way, and I gladly accommodated her wishes!

The Klicka's, old golfing buddies of ours, lived in a two-story townhouse in Elm Grove, a suburb of Milwaukee. Their two bedrooms were on the second floor where we slept. Our bathroom was adjacent to our room near the stairs. Before going to bed one night, I failed to ensure that a night light in the bathroom was turned on. Apparently it was not, for at 2 a.m., I heard a noise that sounded as if someone had fallen down the stairs. I reached for Rita in the bed. She was gone. I jumped up, turned the lights on, and found her at the bottom of the stairs with a slight cut on her head. Indeed, she had fallen down the stairs in search of the bathroom. She seemed okay and came back to bed. Needless to say, I was worried because of her recent meningioma surgery. Dr. Klicka, a dentist with some medical experience, decided that since she reacted favorably to questions that she was probably okay but that she should rest in bed the following day. She did, and I thanked heaven she was able to enjoy the remainder of the trip.

We returned to Louisiana on the night of July 25. Rita insisted that we first see her mother in Rayne before returning to our home. We did, and found her in terrible condition. It was apparent that she had pneumonia. In her misery she did, however, recognize both of us. I suggested that she be brought to the nearby hospital in Crowley for more treatment. We left after an hour or so, and returned to our home in Le Triomphe.

Early the next morning, we received a call from Sepha's doctor informing us that she had just died. At least the home attendants had listened to my comment about the need to get her to the hospital the night before. Rita took the news as well as possible, but we were both so sorry we had been out of town when her mother was in her last days on earth. It must have been hard to be alone. We thought that Rita's brother Harold had been taking care of her, but we doubted it. He had an aversion to visiting in retirement homes and hospitals. He said it reminded him too much of his first wife and her suffering from an incurable disease and a long stay in several hospitals where she eventually died. Sepha's funeral was in Rayne, with the burial in Crowley as planned, adjacent to her departed husband, William, who died years before. It was a huge funeral with so many nearby kin and her many friends in attendance.

A few months later, Rita and I learned of the death of my friend Leo, who had worked with me as an engineer in New Iberia and Texas. He died of a heart attack. Leo was found in his living room sitting in his favorite chair with a newspaper on his lap. Earlier that year in May 1991, he buried his wife, Rexine. Two more of our friends were gone!

Death kept us busy for the next two years. During the previous year followed the progress of Rita's second cousin, Quinn, an army officer, who had been fighting lung cancer for years. Her entire family, with the exception of her mother Cecil, had been members of the US Army. All of her family members were officers, including her father, a veteran of WW II, her brother, a West Point graduate, and her younger sister Cathy. Quinn was buried with full military honors in Crowley. And then later in 1997 and 1998 we attended the funerals of her mother and father. Now only the youngest daughter, Cathy and her brother Sammy, remain in Rita's favorite cousin's family. 1997 and 1998 were years that we attended more funerals of friends and family than any other period.

Rather than focus so much on the death, we visited old friends and entered golf tournaments. In the summer of 1998, we returned to Monroe for a tournament at my old club, Bayou Desiard. It was an enjoyable trip, but I can't brag about winning any prizes during the three days of play. Rita was able to travel; I believed being active helped her. I doubt if her fall in Wisconsin had affected her Alzheimer's; neither did her doctor after an examination when we returned to Lafayette.

CHAPTER XXVII

RITA'S LIFE WITH DEMENTIA

I believe Rita's mother's death affected her more than I initially realized. She was more confused and began roaming more in the neighborhood. I was called several times by neighbors and others to pick her up because she was roaming either on or near the golf course. I had already installed locks on the doors to our clothes closets and the laundry room, for she was attempting to continue her old habit of washing clothes needlessly and rearranging the closets. At times I found wet clothes on the chest of drawers in the bedroom. One day I found a pair of my pants in the kitchen's electric oven when I saw smoke billowing out from the oven a short while after I had started to preheat it. One might have said that this was my fault for not opening the door first. Rita had only mistaken the oven for the clothes dryer. Finally, I regrettably decided that something had to be done to have Rita under a full time watchful eye twenty-four hours a day.

As I mentioned earlier, Rita had been tested by a doctor to determine if her memory was failing. He was afraid it was dementia, which he defined as memory loss and loss of thinking and reasoning capacity in adults. Dementia is also referred to as organic brain syndrome, chronic brain syndrome, hardening of the arteries, senility, and other descriptions. Doctors use the word "dementia," created from two Latin words that mean "away" and "mind" to describe the disease. Dementia does <u>not</u> mean "crazy," although those familiar with it may, at times, come to that conclusion.

One disease that may cause dementia is thyroid disease, of which Rita was a victim. She had been treated for it for many years. Doctor Alois Alzheimer, an early-twentieth-century German physician, was the first to describe the disease named for him. His patient was a woman in her fifties who was diagnosed with the condition originally called pre-senile dementia. Neurologists agree that the dementia, as diagnosed now, is very similar to Dr. Alzheimer's description and so have named it Alzheimer's disease.

Rita's condition was identified and determined by two different MRI procedures which were done to ensure an accurate diagnosis. In my opinion, the medicines given to her proved to be experimental. No cure is available even now, after all these years. Additional experimental procedures are continually being tested as more and more money is allocated and spent on research. The hope is that a cure will soon be found. Meanwhile, thousands of cases are diagnosed each year.

I attempted to learn as much as I could about the subject by reading books describing the nature of the disease, attending classes at Lafayette General Hospital, reading periodicals, contributing to the Alzheimer's Association, soliciting funds for research, and doing anything else I could help. For reading on the subject I suggest *The 36-Hour Day* by Nancy L. Mace, MA, and Peter V. Rabins, MD, MPH, and *The Vanishing Mind* by Leonard L. Heston and June A. White. Both publications were helpful to me in taking care of Rita during her years with dementia.

In April 1997, I learned of a senior daycare service in Lafayette, Chelsea House. It provided daycare for seniors on an hourly basis and was conveniently located. This enabled me to drop Rita off in the morning when I played golf. I could pick her up in four or five hours later with little or no worry. A noon meal was served. The only cost was for the meal and the hours spent there. Aides assisted a registered nurse, who served as the director of the facility. The nurse was experienced and supervised recreation that included card games, coloring and other activities to keep the patients busy. It was salvation for me, but the service was only available from April

15 until May 30, 1997, when they were forced to close for lack of patients and profit. I believe it was the owner's mistake. An hourly rate without a minimum time limit was a poor management decision. I would have gladly paid more for the service.

After that, it was imperative that Rita have someone at home to take care of her while I was away. I contacted the nurse from the senior center, Lisa, whose telephone number suggested she lived near us. I called her, and she was interested in taking Rita into her home or being with her at our home. Lisa started work in June, a week after Chelsea House closed. Rita enjoyed being with her, and Lisa enjoyed Rita's company. At times they would shop together, take rides together, eat lunch together, and just generally enjoyed one another's company. Some thought they were daughter and mother. The arrangement was only for five days a week, and I was at home and "on duty" on the weekends.

I remember August 31, 1997, when Rita and I visited her brother Harold and his wife Stella in Rayne. Harold was under the care of two friends of Stella's, who were living with them. He had a heart condition and was under the care of a physician in Rayne. He was on a number of medications that permitted him to live a normal life even though he was seventy-seven years old and was somewhat overweight. On that particular Saturday afternoon, Harold was acting strangely. To me I thought that he might have been in a coma judging by the way he was talking, but no one agreed with me, so I let it go.

On the way home Rita and I discussed Harold's questionable condition and decided it might not be serious, but early the next morning, Stella's niece, who lived next door, called us with the news that Harold had died that night in the American Legion Hospital in nearby Crowley. She went on to say that after we had left Saturday, he was given a number of his pills with a glass of water, which he threw up. An ambulance was called, and he was brought to the hospital. He died there later gasping for breath. It was a shock to us all when I called to inform Harold's aunts and cousins.

Rita, I doubt, realized what had happened. At the funeral home the next day, she seemed as if it was a social, not a funeral. I don't recall her shedding a tear, but she had been very close to her only brother. I know it must have been her dementia. Harold was buried in Rayne having died, according to the doctor's death certificate, of congestive heart failure.

Lisa had been taking care of Rita for almost a year. It was the summer of 1998 when she told us that she and her family were going on a vacation to her husband's home in Virginia. They expected to be gone for several weeks. Meanwhile, my friends, believing they were helping me, suggested I look into K Place, a new retirement home for Rita that was under construction in the southwest part of Lafayette. I did; I attended their promotional meetings where they outlined their experience and bragged about how great their services were. Their rates were comparable to other places, so I reserved a room for Rita beginning Monday, March 1, 1999. Later it was to become one of the saddest days of my life.

I should have questioned the experience of local personnel, for they were adamant about my not visiting Rita for the first three days of her arrival to the facilities. They called it a "settling down period." She was assigned to a room with another patient. I called the home each day to ask how she was, and they always said she was adjusting satisfactorily.

Finally, on Thursday, the third day of her confinement, I went to see her. She was not in the sitting area, so I walked around the building into several halls where I heard someone beating on a wall in the next hall. I turned the corner and saw that it was Rita trying to open a door into the surrounding grounds.

I hardly recognized her. She looked as if she had not slept since her arrival; the circles under her eyes told me that. She, however, recognized me immediately; we hugged and kissed. I asked her what had happened, but she had no answer. I suggested we go to her room, and I put her to bed. She went to sleep right away. I had a serious conversation with the supervisor, who offered no excuse for letting Rita run wild all by herself. She did admit that the only time Rita enjoyed anything was when she was taken for a ride on their bus. I suggested that they give her more attention, because Rita needed help since she had no idea where she was or why she was not with me. The supervisor said they would try to do better. It was evident there were no planned activities as advertised.

I returned again the next afternoon shortly after lunch to visit Rita. When I saw her, she seemed much better and was more herself again. I left feeling better, but that feeling didn't last long. Later that night, at about 11:30, I was awakened by a call from the home. "Miss Rita has gone berserk. We are taking her to Lafayette General for an examination," the caller announced.

I asked, "What did she do to act that way, and why take her to a hospital?"

"She hit a pregnant aide in the stomach as she was trying to take a soda away from her. We have no other choice but to take her to the hospital," continued the caller.

"What? Rita does not go around hitting people. Why didn't the aide give her the drink to satisfy her?" I responded.

The conversation ended unsettled, and with that I dressed and sped to Lafayette General Hospital, arriving a few minutes before the ambulance. When Rita saw me, she gave me a big wave and one of her great smiles. I could see nothing was wrong with her. After an examination by the doctor, I asked the nurse, "How can I get Rita out of the hospital, since there is nothing wrong with her?"

The nurse agreed with my assessment and said, "Just sign this release and you can take her home."

I did, and once there Rita slept like a log until after 10 a.m. the next day, and most of all, she was so happy to be at home again; so was I.

The next day Rita and I drove to K. Place where I gathered up her clothes and medicine. I told the supervisor, "I am taking Rita home with me, and I want back every penny that I paid you for her stay, including the funds to the end of the month. It was a week of hell for both of us. Do you people know what you are doing?"

She said, "The money must come from our office in Chicago. I will contact them."

It took a month, but I did receive the one month's advance I had paid them. I understand, too, that the so-called pregnant aide Rita had allegedly hit was okay, and nothing was wrong with her. Rita had never hit anyone during our married life. It was not her nature. It was ridiculous that Rita had been treated so badly by an inexperienced group. They were lucky I did not sue them for defamation of character, misleading advertising, or any other number of things. I wonder, too, what happened to the head nurse there, who apparently was not trained for the position. She should have been replaced for lack of knowledge.

Rita was taking Aricept, a medication that seemed to help her memory and disposition. I took care of her until Lisa returned from her vacation. With Lisa, who was highly experienced, Rita was fine, and I was happy to raise Lisa's hourly rate. In the ensuing weeks Lisa was in and out of our house as well as her own, having some sickness in the family. Again, with Lisa's problems, I took care of Rita.

I soon learned that Rita was not interested in visiting her hairdresser because she objected to having her hair washed by the beautician. The beautician suggested we see a barber, Kenny, for whom she formerly worked. We did, and he proved to be a lifesaver because Kenny not only trimmed Rita's hair, but he also did mine and continues since Rita met her maker.

In July, my urologist found that my prostate readings were on the upward movement which, if the levels of PSA reached a rating of five or higher, would require me to take other medicines. He recommended treatment with Lupron. Because MD Anderson in Houston started my treatment of prostate cancer, I asked if my local doctor had any objection if I saw my doctor there when he prescribed the Lupron. He had no objection and agreed to watch my problem closely.

Meanwhile, I had spoken to my state representative about the way K. Place handled Rita's stay there. She was interested in working on guidelines for retirement homes and asked if I would help her. I agreed, but she must have dropped the project because I never heard from her again after that contact.

Lisa and Misty, a new caretaker, were now both staying with Rita. It was a good arrangement, for Rita liked both, and their visits made my life more routine. I was doing the cooking and taking care of Rita each night until one of the girls relieved me the next morning. Misty did not stay with Rita long because she found a job at a department store. Lisa was then once again my steady employee when available.

The summer went on with little change, and I managed to have available help for Rita when I needed it. At other times I was the caretaker and did not dislike it. I was with my love who simply could not take care of herself. If I were in her condition and she was okay, she would have found a way to care for me. That, I believe, is what love is about. I remember the vows at our wedding. I had answered "I will" to the minister when he'd asked, "Wilt thou have this woman to be thou wedded wife, to live together after God's ordinance in the holy estate of matrimony? Wilt thou love her, comfort her, honor, and keep her in sickness and in health and, forsaking all others, so long as ye both shall live?"

Rita also answered "I will" when asked the same question by the minister. I adhered to it, and I am sure she, too, would have done the same had the opportunity presented itself. There was no question in either of our minds; we would care for one another.

At Christmastime, for a change of scenery, I made a reservation for a three-day holiday at the Grand Hotel in Point Clear, Alabama, across the bay from Mobile. I had heard that Christmas dinners there were fabulous. In addition, there was a golf course available for play. We arrived on Christmas Eve, looked the place over, and settled down in our room in a building adjacent to the nearby original hotel that was built in the 1800s. Rita was somewhat confused, but she had always loved to go places. The first night she was not interested in going to bed, and I had trouble keeping her in the room. She wanted to walk in the hall! I finally got her to bed, and I do believe she slept a few hours before wanting to go elsewhere again.

In the morning we dressed and had breakfast, and then I took her for a ride around the grounds before stopping at the golf course. She let me know that she had no desire to watch me play golf or even ride in a cart with me. Golf, therefore, was quickly eliminated as an activity option during the rest of our stay!

A couple from Franklinton, Louisiana, who had spent several Christmases at this hotel, became our acquaintances. I explained Rita's condition, and they readily understood the situation. We had dinner with them the first night and arranged to have Christmas dinner with them the following afternoon, to be served in a large dining area on the grounds. We met as planned. All went well until dinner was served. Rita wanted dark turkey meat, but she was served white meat. She complained so much I quickly sought the waiter to have it changed. I knew then how confused and unhappy she was. After dinner, before going back to our room for a nap, I suggested that we walk around the grounds. It was a quick walk for Rita. She was not happy at all about anything we did. We went back to the room and, with some encouragement, she took a nap. Upon awaking, her attitude was much better.

The next day we checked out of the hotel and went downtown for a barbeque luncheon, which we both enjoyed. On the way home later that night there was a small sleet storm from Mobile to Baton Rouge. I decided that if it continued into Baton Rouge we would stop there rather than drive in it all the way back to Lafayette. Luckily, the storm eased as we entered Baton Rouge, so we drove home to Lafayette and Le Triomphe in clear weather. The trip was enjoyable to a point. From the experience I concluded that Rita was becoming easily confused, and it would have been better had we remained at home. The change from home was too new to her and possibly a reminder her of experience somewhere "different" at K. Place. For future holidays we remained at home where all was familiar to her.

In January 1998, my doctor found my PSA was rising from 3.5 to 5.0 and suggested a bone scan to ensure that the cancer had not spread. Thank heavens, the scan was negative.

Brother Bill, called from San Antonio to determine if I was interested in purchasing the 1998 Cadillac he had rented and was about to turn in. With only twenty thousand miles on the odometer, I thought it was a good buy and agreed on a price. Two of our close friends, Al and Dot, informed us that they were planning a trip through San Antonio and offered Rita and me a ride to pick up the car at Bill's. We accepted their invitation, visited with Bill and Juanita, bought the car and, several days later, on February 25, 2000, started home. The trip went as well as expected, with Rita not knowing exactly what was going on. Being a victim of incontinence, she required several diaper changes driving to San Antonio, but she could not understand why we had stopped at so many gas stations. I sorely missed Lisa on the trip, but we made it okay even with Rita's questioning. I remember after a service station stop on the way home she leaned over to me as we returned to the car and said seriously,

"Jim, thank you so much for taking me with you. I enjoyed it very much."

I did not know what to say, but I did try to convince her who I was. It frightened me, for after fifty- three years of married life, she acted as if she did not know that I was her husband. It was a shock. But I said, "Sweetie-Pie, don't you remember we have been married over fifty-three years and have moved together all over the country and even Australia! I guess you are tired so we will stop in Houston for the night and see some old neighbors who now live there. I know you will enjoy seeing them."

A few more miles down the road before we reached Houston, she seemed more relaxed. I stopped at a motel for a room just off the highway in Houston. Later it seemed she remembered me and was her old self again, but the motel became another problem since it wasn't her bed. With some coaxing, I finally got her to sleep. The next morning all was ok. At times, her memory left her, the aftermath of confusion. I do believe that when she became tired, it was worse. I don't recall her ever acting as she did before our stop in Houston -- not knowing who I was. The next day she was okay when we visited friends. She probably had been tired the night before which is why she forgot who I was.

On May 8, 2000, I decided Rita would be better off in a first-class retirement home. Her caretaker, Lisa, was fine, but her availability was not always dependable because of her family obligations. I was at her mercy because she had a young family of her own. So I investigated Stone Village in Lafayette, a retirement home that accepted dementia patients. I made a reservation for Rita, since there were no rooms available at the time. It is an old, established home, though, and one of the most recommended in Lafayette.

Before we received a date to enter Stone Village, I heard of a doctor who had had success in treating Alzheimer's patients using herbs and so forth. Perhaps I was grasping at straws, but I let him examine Rita. He suggested other tests. Not having too much faith in his expertise, I suggested he get approval from Medicare before any further treatments or examinations were made. He was unsuccessful in getting Medicare approval; therefore, our visits with him were curtailed—and at just the right time, particularly when he suggested herbal treatments with exorbitant prices for the medicines. I know now it would have been money sent down the drain. At the time, though, I would have tried anything to revive Rita's memory and have her normal again.

It turned out that I was not too early in making a reservation at the retirement home, for Lisa let me know shortly thereafter that she and her family were planning a two-week vacation in Hawaii. Misty, my other sitter, was still on call, but she was having problems with her small daughter, so I became Rita's full-time caretaker once more.

It took several days to complete the medical examinations of Rita's condition prior to entering Stone Village, but we managed to meet all the requirements just prior to entry. Chest x-rays, TB inoculation, and skin tests were all needed. The arrangement was more satisfying than at K. Place, for I was now dealing with an organization that I believed cared for their patients as well as one that followed established state and federal rules.

On July 17, 2000, Rita entered Stone Village in a much better frame of mind than K-Y the former home. I sat with her for lunch the first day and asked Lisa to meet her for lunch the second day. She did, and the transition was great compared to K. Place and the problems we had there. Each succeeding day thereafter when I visited Rita, I could see the improvement in her attitude. My desire to have her at home was waived somewhat since she seemed to be adjusting to the new surroundings. And secondly, I had not made a diligent search for aides on a permanent basis. Lisa and Misty were more or less available when I needed them. With Rita adapting as well as she was, I felt that now I had all the dependable and trained personnel I needed.

It took time for Rita to completely acclimate herself, but she did so within a few weeks. I visited her each day at about 3 pm, when she usually awoke from her nap. We would take a walk, have refreshments, and talk a lot. When dinner was served at about 5, I usually left for home. On other days I was always available to drive her to her doctor appointments. It still took her a few weeks to completely settle down. I could tell from the circles under her eyes that she did not always sleep enough. Also, she must have fallen at one point and bruised her hip. But typically, no one seemed to know what happened.

Barbara, the social director, was our favorite. She ran the daily entertainment for patients in the solarium. She was adept at keeping all the patients busy when they were in her charge. On Fridays, "big-time entertainment" was presented in a separate area of the home. The large dining room, normally used by those living in adjacent apartments, was the site of outside entertainment. Local Cajun entertainers including bands, comedians, and other local artists performed to the delight of the patients. Rita and I were not fond of Cajun music, but we listened occasionally. Birthdays were massive celebrations there, with cake and refreshments for all.

Additionally, there was an exercise yard where Rita and I walked daily, weather permitting. She enjoyed it very much, and we both liked being alone together for a while. On occasion I took her for a car ride and on Sundays and other holidays, I always brought her home for lunch or dinner. I tried to follow Rita's daily routine by letting her nap after lunch before I would take her back for dinner at Stone Village. It was a pleasant outing for her, which we enjoyed very much. I particularly did not want her to forget her home.

In November, Rita's neurologist prescribed a new medicine, Exelon. He increased the number of milligrams from the 1.5 mg, in two week intervals, up to a maximum of 4.45 mg. She was under close observation because the medicine was new on the market. At first after taking the medicine, when walking, Rita seemed to lean to the right and was not too stable. After a few weeks, though, she was able to walk in her usual manner. The medicine seemed to help her memory, but it was not intended as a cure. There were no cures on the market.

On November 11, 2000, when I arrived I noticed that Rita was catching a cold. With each succeeding visit, the cold seemed to get worse. I asked the nurse to check her thoroughly after she vomited one day. Rita's face was very red, and she had a temperature of 106 degrees. I immediately suggested she be hospitalized, for I feared pneumonia. An ambulance was called, and we were in Lafayette General Hospital a half hour later. Rita and I were in the emergency room until 4 the next morning, when we were finally moved into a room. A tube was placed in her nose to drain fluid from her lungs.

After a number of checks, it was determined that she had aspiration from the new medicine and a urinary infection in addition to pneumonia. Her heart was also checked with an echocardiogram. A decision was made to change to Seroquel and discontinue Exelon. The following day, Rita was somewhat better, but a number of tests were ordered. The pneumonia cleared up, and she returned to Stone Village on December 12. Upon her arrival she was unable to walk very well, but she gained strength each day.

By Christmas, Rita was okay. I picked her up and brought her home. She opened presents and ate some of her Christmas dinner, but not enthusiastically. After lunch, I put her to bed. She slept till 4 pm, at which time I brought her back to Stone Village. When she got out of the car and walked to her room, I noticed that she took short, short steps, but at home she walked very well. Was she trying to tell me something? Thankfully the next day when I visited her, she was okay.

It was the beginning of a new year, and I continued my daily visits with Rita. It was very heartening to me that each time she saw me, she knew who I was. She was usually in her room when I arrived, sometimes asleep, but I did not wake her for fear she may have needed all the rest she could get. The aides usually dressed her, but at times I did prior to our daily walk down the hall to the door leading into the yard where we could walk and talk. There were benches where we sometimes sat and talked a while before going into the solarium for cookies and a drink with the other patients. As we walked in holding hands, we could hear some say, "Here come the lovers." And it was so true- we were still lovers. This pleased me very much, for I believe our love for one another was still evident. We both showed it, and it never changed in our more than fifty-eight years of married life and being together.

On my next visit with Rita and her neurologist, he agreed to help me obtain a handicapped placard for my car. It helped very much when Rita was with me, for handicapped parking zones were always nearer building entrances and doctors' offices.

In January, I was careful not to spread a cold I had acquired. I did see Rita but did not kiss her as I normally did. Not wishing to give her or any of the other residents a cold, I kept my visitations short and tried not to touch anyone. I missed Rita's kisses, but the cold was soon gone, and everything was routine thereafter.

Life continued at Stone Village, but I began to notice that the aides were not as attentive as I expected. I noticed on many occasions that Rita was not always changed and left with wet pants on for hours. She continued to have bad coughs with little relief.

Then one day I informed the nurse at Stone Village that I had appointments for Rita with two doctors: one to check her hemorrhoids, which were giving her problems, and the other to check her cough. The first doctor said that the hemorrhoids were okay. There was no need for an operation, but her condition should be watched. The cough, her other doctor decided, was an allergy and was also to be watched.

On Easter Sunday I picked Rita up for dinner at home. The way she ate my baked duck made me want to bring her home at once and keep her with me again. It was constantly on my mind to do so. She always smiled at home, which made me realize that she, too, wanted to be with me again. When Easter was over, I returned her to Stone Village once more.

The next Tuesday, my allergies were so bad I did not visit with Rita very long. I felt so bad that I left her before supper. My condition continued for the balance of the week. I did see her every day but did not spend as much time as I would have liked because of the allergies. On Sunday when I visited with her, she was in bed sleeping, but she woke up shortly after I arrived. When she saw me, she said, "I love you."

I was so happy to hear her say that that my allergy faded away, and I replied, "I love you, too, Miss Sweetie Pie."

She smiled so pretty. I dressed her, and we went for our usual walk down the hall into the yard and finally into the solarium for cookies and a drink. Shortly thereafter, I did some small thing for her, and she surprised me with, "Thank you." I believe she had recovered, if only temporarily.

The next day I took Rita to have the nosepiece on her eyeglasses replaced. Riding in the car was very pleasant, for she was very talkative and noticed things along the way as we drove past them. It seemed she was more like her old self again-so interested in the scenery.

Later it was time for her checkup with our doctor. During each visit there were problems to overcome. She refused several times to open her mouth for examination, but the doctor was able to take most of her vital signs and decided she was okay. He also spent time with me and recommended a cough syrup, because I was bothered with a cold, allergy, or something. The medicine that he prescribed gave me great relief.

I was informed that while sitting at the dinner table at Stone Village, Rita threw paper napkins at other patients. I could not understand why. Those I spoke with had no answers. As a consequence of these actions, she was given Depocanc, a depressant, to calm her down. I was not in agreement with the decision, but something had to be done to curtail her mischievous energy and keep her quiet at the dinner table. When she was with me, she was fine, but I had to rely on those who were with her to tell me what she did when I wasn't there. Usually when we were together, she enjoyed talking to and smiling with the other patients. I could not imagine her throwing paper napkins at the table.

I later heard from the wife of another patient that the monthly rate for patients was being increased by several hundred dollars per month because of Medicare's increase; however Stone Village did not admit Medicare patients and had nothing to do with Medicare. With that knowledge, I wrote to the owner of the company questioning the reason for such an increase in monthly rates. It was the second increase since Rita had been there.

Within a few days, the owner and I met in his office to discuss the contents of my letter. He said, "My rates are going up since I understand Medicare is increasing their payments."

"But you don't rely on Medicare payments," I replied.

He and I had a short, heated discussion before I was able to get the truth out of him. I finally got him to tell the real reason. "Expenses," he said, "are rising, and labor is costing me more."

"Why didn't you just say that instead of the Medicare excuse?" I asked.

Our conversation ended cordially, and we both agreed to keep one another informed of future increases. The increase stood, however, and I seriously considered bringing Rita home immediately, but I also realized that making arrangements for experienced help would be necessary before I moved her.

About the same time, I learned that Rita's brother's wife, Stella, had died in Rayne. I was still suffering from a cold or whatever my condition, coupled with the lack of sleep, but I managed to attend the wake the night before the funeral. Unfortunately I was unable to attend the funeral; my condition hadn't improved.

The nurse had no explanation for Rita's earache or why she had swelling. Finally, I took Rita to our doctor, who decided nothing was wrong; it was probably wax or water from the shower that had gotten into her ear. He believed all would be okay in a few days. He also decided then that all tests on me were negative and suggested I take a depressant for sleeping. It worked, and I finally was able to get a good night's sleep after many weeks of tossing and turning.

While my problem was being corrected, Nurse April found a rash on Rita's buttocks and between her legs. I blamed it on aides not changing her during the day when she was wet. They, instead, decided it was probably caused by the antibiotics she was taking for her ear. I could never determine exactly where that medicine came from, since the doctor had not given a prescription for her ear. He'd said everything was normal—more lies or untruths! After applying salve to the affected areas, the home staff dressed her, and we made our routine walk down the hall, into the yard, and finally back inside the solarium for cookies and a drink. Rita walked as usual and had no complaints about the rash. Even in these days she seldom complained; nothing seemed to bother her! Always believing I could do better for Rita, one of the patient's daughters and I discussed the possibility of renting a large home where she lived, and starting our own home for elders. She thought it was a good idea and asked her husband, an accountant, to investigate the feasibility of such a venture. He did and later advised that he did not think the investment would be a financial success. Labor would also be a constant problem. I agreed, and further discussions stopped.

During the days that followed, Rita was subjected to Troy, a newly hired, ill-mannered male nurse. Once I witnessed his attempt to give her medicine. He called her to get her attention and then crammed a spoonful of medicine into her mouth. Before she had time to swallow it, he attempted to fill another spoonful of Depocane and similarly crammed it down her throat. She rebelled and pushed his hand away, as any sane person would do, spilling it on her clean sweater. Sitting there watching, I said, "What in the hell are you trying to do, gag her? Let her swallow first!"

With that he handed me the spoon and said, "Here, you give it to her!"

I discussed the situation with the manager the next day. We did not see Tony around after that one incident. He was dangerous serving patients with dementia. Why he was hired in the first place was a question in my mind.

The Sunday following, I picked Rita up for dinner at home. The drive was pleasant, and she was very attentive. When we arrived, though, she acted as if she had never been there before. She walked over the entire house, inspecting each room, but said nothing. I wish I could have read her mind, for I was sure she knew something about each room. She had arranged the furniture and everything when we moved in.

After dinner, we both went to bed for a nap. She did not sleep. I almost did. When we returned to Stone Village that evening, we found only three aides working. Again, I was tempted to take Rita back home with me. Stone Village, at times, lacked the personnel to care for their twenty or more patients. I later decided against it, but the thought remained.

On Monday everything was normal. There were an adequate number of aides available to care for the patients. Tuesday I took Rita to have her hair cut. She was groggy when I picked her up but was okay in the barbershop. I held her hand as Kenny, the barber, did his job. She was very quiet when I brought her back to the home but became her old self after taking her medicine.

Wednesday and Thursday were bad days for Rita. When I saw her, the circles under her eyes indicated that she had not slept very well the preceding nights. On the third afternoon, she acted like her old self again, talking and smiling. I attributed it to a good night's sleep, even though the nurse said she was still suffering from her other ailments, such as enlarged hemorrhoids.

On June 5, 2001, the sky opened up and the rain poured during my visit with Rita. I had no idea how the weather would affect my drive home. Rita was fine, and we had our usual happy, talkative afternoon. I left Stone Village that afternoon about 4:30 in the pouring rain and decided to drive home via Youngsville to avoid the slow traffic on Highway 90. Driving through water a foot deep on Highway 92 in Youngsville, I was able to get within a block of Highway 90, only a quarter mile from home. Just before reaching the intersection, the coulee crossing Highway 92 was so deep that the road was closed, and I was unable to reach Highway 90 and home. I detoured to Broussard and entered Highway 90 near the railroad overpass and headed south on my way home. As I approached Highway 92 on my right, I noticed a stream of cars stopped in both the southbound and northbound lanes. It was evident that the same coulee blocking Highway 92 was also blocking Highway 90. The water was just too deep to drive through, so the road was closed. I managed to turn around and drive back to Lafayette where I called friends Al and Dot, who suggested I spend the night with them. I did.

The next day after breakfast I was able to drive home, where I showered, dressed, and returned to see Rita. She was in bed but not sleeping soundly. I read the paper as she napped for a while. Her hemorrhoids were being treated with suppositories, and I thought that helped her sleep better.

Over the next three months, I visited Rita regularly in the afternoons. Some days I found her asleep, other days I found her suspended on restraining straps when she needed more control. Her doctor had changed her dosage of Aricept, which seemed to help her memory and general attitude. At times she was her old self—happy, talkative, smiling, and very lovable. Her sight in her right eye was deteriorating, and later it was diagnosed as macular degeneration. Never did she complain of not seeing well with that eye. Perhaps she accepted it as well as she had accepted her dementia.

Generally, Rita had her good days as well as her bad days at Stone Village. While I believe the attention given her could have been better, I do believe it was acceptable the majority of the time. Her nurse continued to help her as much as she could. I did notice that her roommate screamed occasionally when I was there. If she yelled in the middle of the night, this may have affected Rita's ability to sleep and be the reason for the circles under her eyes. I asked that Rita be transferred to another room when one was available. At the time, there were no vacancies. The change never occurred; her roommate unfortunately died a few months later. By that time Rita had been living at Stone Village exactly one year.

Meanwhile, my urologist, who was recording my rising PSA levels, gave me a report to send to my doctor at MD Anderson in Houston, who had operated on me several years before. Because my reading was somewhat higher than before, he thought I might have to take a trip to Houston to discuss it with them.

In July, Rita and I visited her neurologist, who noted how she had improved and therefore planned to reduce her tranquilizers, which were causing her to be so sleepy at times. We both agreed that the retirement home would rather keep their patients on dope to make their jobs easier. I could vividly see the difference between when Rita was on dope and when she wasn't.

Within a few days I knew she was her old self when she called me "Bo" as I walked into her room. Reducing the dosage of her tranquilizers really was good for her! She had not called me that in years! "Bo" was her nickname for me after we were first married, many years ago. I was pleased that the medicine was causing a miracle and she was being cured. Later I learned it was only a temporary improvement. No such luck for a permanent change!

July 30, 2001, was the first day in a long time that I did not go to Stone Village to visit with Rita. That morning I had a dilation of my esophagus at my doctor's office. He had sedated me for the procedure and said I should not drive for twenty-four hours. Bob, a golfing buddy, drove me to and from the doctor. I did call Stone Village to check on Rita to determine if she was okay or in need of anything. All was fine.

The next day, Rita was as happy to see me as I was to see her. Her first words were, "I want to go with you!"

She held my hand tightly and would not let go. Two aides came in to change her. They were very rough with her, and I asked, "Aren't you going to brush her teeth?"

One replied, "They did it after lunch."

"Then why are the toothbrushes so dry?" I asked. No answer from either one.

Later I told the supervisor about the dry toothbrush, for what it was worth. Rita was also very sleepy throughout my visit, which I believed was caused by the administered dope she received.

The next day was about the same; Rita held my hand and hated to let it go. We were both happy to see one another. We walked down the hall into the yard where Rita found a chair and sat down. She seemed agitated and asked me, "Why am I here?"

I told her, "It's because your memory is not always too good and I can't take care of you every day at home. These people here have more time to wait on you and see that you are fed properly. And most of all, to be sure you take your medicine. Don't you like it here?"

She had no more to say. I dropped the subject, but I believed she understood what I'd said. Later, Nurse April told me that the doctor had only lowered her Synthroid dosage for her thyroid problem, which may have caused her disposition change the last few days that continued into the following week when she continued to be her old, jolly self.

On occasion Rita and I ventured into the assisted living area of Stone Village, located in the same building. I was surprised to see Rita being so friendly with five elderly ladies who sat in the dining room with her. Rita walked up to them, sat down, and began a conversation with each one. She seemed to enjoy the visit as well as they did. For Rita, they were so different from the dementia patients she saw every day. The women were there because of age, not dementia, and they knew us from our previous walks in the area. They enjoyed seeing Rita as much as she seeing them.

In later weeks I learned that several aides had found that Rita hated to expose her body to unfamiliar aides who attempted to bathe her or even change her briefs. Perhaps she must have been living in another time of her life, when she was more aware of her privacy. Otherwise, she was talkative and when I said I would pick her up on Sunday to take her home, she replied, "I'll be ready tomorrow. I love you."

I replied, "I love you too, Miss Sweetie Pie." She smiled so prettily. I then left for home, sad that she was not coming with me.

Rita was just as loving when I picked her up the next morning for her Sunday visit at home with me. When we reached home, Lisa called to say she planned to visit Rita at Stone Village. I suggested she and her son, Timmy, come over to our house for lunch. They did, and we had a great time! Rita seemed to enjoy their company so much. We were such good friends. Later that day, it was hard for me to take Rita back to Stone Village.

Monday, after I picked her up and seated her in the car, she again surprised me with, "Thank you."

After Labor Day I had to return to MD Anderson in Houston for a checkup. It was only a one-day trip. I left Lafayette at 4 a.m. one morning on Highway I-10 along with every truck in America, it seemed. Even so, I arrived in Houston by 7 a.m. after being on what seemed to be a race track with so many trucks traveling fast. I could not drive less than eighty miles per hour without the risk of being run over, so the four-hour trip only took three. I definitely returned home at a slower rate after my visit with my doctor there, arriving in Lafayette by 7 that evening. Rita was already in bed. I said a few words to her, picked up her dirty clothes, and went home for a good night's rest.

When I arrived the next afternoon, Rita was not in her bed. The aides said I had asked that they keep Rita up this day (I had not!). I found her in the solarium sleeping in a chair. I know I had not mentioned anything about keeping her up. Perhaps my not being there the previous day had made Rita perturbed after I left for Houston or something similar that caused a mix-up in her daily routine. I soon learned how hard it was to find out why some things happened at Stone Village.

A nurse called me later at home later that day to tell me Rita had taken off her glasses and had calmly broken them in half. Why, I never did learn. The next day, I took her glasses to be repaired and learned that they were guaranteed to be unbreakable. The store sent them back to the factory, and Rita was without glasses for a week or so, but the glasses were repaired free of charge. That guarantee was first-rate.

Several weeks later, a Cajun band played in the main dining room. Rita and I went in to listen with the other patients. After the band played a few songs, Rita leaned over and asked, "Why are we here listening to that noise?"

Neither she nor I especially cared for the Cajun music. We got up, walked a while, and entered her side of the building and the solarium where it was nice and quiet. We talked for some time before I left her for home. With behaviors like this, I often questioned whether Rita was actually affected with dementia; at other times I knew, based on some of her other behaviors.

We celebrated Rita's seventy-eighth birthday on October 19. I brought a large pineapple cake and a new shirt for her. She enjoyed being at the head of the table with the other patients, eating the cake with her fork and her two hands. Our friend Al came with a nice birthday card. I know Rita was happy because she could not stop talking. I hated to leave her that evening. She always enjoyed birthday parties, large or small, and this one was a large one where she was the star.

I also remember the month of October as being dominated by an Alzheimer's drive for money. I canvassed my senior golf association membership for contributions. I even contacted others I knew on the Internet. My collection totaled over twelve- hundred dollars. Later at the Alzheimer's Walk held in a local park, Stone Village and I received a prize for collecting the largest donation. I was unable to participate in the walk because of my lingering cold, but we enjoyed watching the participants. I understand Stone Village has framed the picture of me receiving the award with others from the retirement-home. Rita was up and down during the next few months. Some days she was radiant and talkative. Other times she was sleepy and acted as if doped, which I believed was the case. However, I was happy she was able to attend my eightieth birthday party on January 19. It was a luncheon party at the club for my golfing buddies, their wives, my brother Bill, his wife Juanita, her mother, and my non-golfing friend, Horace, and his wife Etta Mae. It was a lovely affair for the twelve of us. Rita was her old self even though she may not have remembered most of the attendees. Regardless, she acted very satisfied and was her ladylike self once more. Everyone marveled how well she was.

Later Rita and I had supper at home with Bill, Juanita, and Bill's mother-in law, who spent the night at my house. I regret that I had to take Rita back to Stone Village later that night after a busy day, particularly when I returned the next day (Sunday) to pick her up for lunch at home again.

The following months were more of the same with me making daily afternoon visits to be with Rita. I do believe we both looked forward to seeing one another that way. I am positive I was! In February, I asked Lisa to visit Rita and determine if she thought it wise for me to consider removing her from Stone Village and bringing her home so we could be together again. Of course I would have adequate help around the house to maintain her. Lisa suggested, after some thought, that I bring her home at first for several overnight stays to observe her behavior being at home again. I never did.

The following day, February 2, 2002, I received an early morning call from Stone Village. They told me that they could not wake Rita. She was breathing normally, and her vital signs were fine. They also had called our doctor, who advised them to send her to the hospital at once. I dressed and reached the hospital just as Rita did in the ambulance. She was awake and alert.

The doctors checked her from head to foot with a blood test, CAT scan, chest x-ray, and heart cardiogram together with recording her blood pressure, heartbeat, for a complete examination. They could find nothing wrong and concluded it might have been a seizure, since blood had come from her mouth. Blood was also on the sheet of her bed.

Rita was released after a few hours, but first we acquired two hospital gowns to cover her since they had brought her in her night clothes from Stone Village. I then drove her back to the home in the only clothes she had- hospital gowns. Upon our return, she was placed back in bed and served breakfast.

Later that day, sometime after breakfast, two new aides attempted to take Rita's vital signs without success. Rita resisted their efforts. The aides had not known of her hospital visit earlier that day so I got her out of bed and dressed her. Thank goodness, she was all right when I saw her later that day. I did wonder how well-informed the aides were. Lines of communication at the home appeared to be nonexistent, and I called this to their attention once again. Their lack of communication was uncalled for.

Because Rita was dressed, I walked her into the solarium, where she sat and rested in a lounge chair. It was a hectic day, but thank heavens, she was okay. It was hard for her to speak. She could not remember the proper words.

A seizure, I learned, was a sudden episode of uncontrolled activity in the brain. If the abnormal activity remains confined to one area, the patient might experience tingling or twitching of only a small area of the body, such as the face or an extremity. If the abnormal electrical activity spreads throughout the brain, consciousness is lost and a "grand mal" seizure results. Seizures may be caused, I learned, by many different neurological or medical problems, including injury to the brain. I concluded that this seizure could have been caused by the meningioma operation she had had years ago. I understood also that one might bite one's tongue during a seizure, which may have been the source of the blood on her face, shirt, and bed.

A few weeks later on February 22, 2002, I received a call from Stone Village that Rita had apparently had another seizure at breakfast. She was taken to the hospital. I arrived ten minutes before the ambulance. When I saw her, her face and shirt were bloody. Checks of her blood pressure, heartbeat, and breathing were made, just like the last time. All were normal. The doctor prescribed Dilantin in minimum doses to begin with, then in increased amounts to prevent further seizures. A personal therapist friend of ours worked with her walking and thought it best for us to assist her walking. In time, she was able to walk as well as before. I had no idea it would take so long, but between assisting her to walk and the use of a walker and wheelchair, Rita was back to normal by early April.

Around this time, I brought another incident to the attention of the director of nursing. I had been called, later in April, by a kitchen helper, who said she had found Rita sitting on the floor in the solarium. How she got there, no one knew. She could have fallen from the chair or tripped; since there were no supervisors or aides there when the situation occurred, it was anybody's guess. All supervisors had been attending a safety meeting, and not one aide or anyone in authority was in the solarium with the twenty or so patients. I advised the supervisor, "It is a must for someone to be with your dementia patients at all times."

I was assured it would not happen again. My patience was running out more each day with the lack of adequate help and neglect that was so visible at times. With such lack of attention, I wanted Rita at home with me, so I again decided I would try to find experienced, dependable help. I told the staff that someone must be with Rita at all times.

But a similar accident happened to me the following Sunday at home as I was changing Rita's wet diaper. I left her lying on the bed while I went into the bathroom for a towel. When I returned, she was on the floor. I quickly learned how easily it was for her to fall off a bed or chair. Thank heavens she was getting tough and there were no bruises or any damage. After changing her, we moved back into our living room for popcorn and TV. She didn't so much as complain about the fall. Her only complaint was about returning to Stone Village. I could see that she hated to return to that place after having dinner with me. Once she said she wanted to stay at home. Then, as we were leaving the house to go back to Stone Village, as she passed our dining room table, she ran her fingers over it and looked at me with regretful eyes that said, "I doubt if I will ever see this table again." I assured her she would. It was heartbreaking to see her that way. The table was hers; she had selected it and purchased it herself many years ago!

In June Rita had an appointment with her doctor, who marveled at her good condition. He mentioned that she would surely outlive me. Those words were music to my ears, but unfortunately that did not materialize! Several days later, it was time to visit Rita's neurologist, who also thought she was getting along so well. At the same time, the neurologist suggested that Rita would be better off in Stone Village than at home. I did not argue with him but also did not agree.

July 17, 2002, was Rita's two-year anniversary at Stone Village. I found her asleep at 1:30 in the afternoon. The aides woke her to give her a "silver bullet" medication for her terrible bleeding hemorrhoids. They thought she should have a wheelchair, which I was against. I knew if she had one, no one except me would ever walk her. I knew full well that she was still capable of walking. Finally, I agreed to secure a wheelchair, but only with the understanding that it only be used temporarily. She was to walk unassisted as much as possible each day.

Several days later I spoke with Connie, who was doing private sitting at Stone Village, about the possibility of her working for me when I brought Rita home. Connie, who was not happy with Stone Village rules, said she was ready for a change. She said that she had been providing this type of work for years and had a list of aides who were very dependable. We agreed on an hourly fee, and Connie agreed to start work in my home on September1. After being assured of capable help, I informed Stone Village in writing, as required in our contract, that Rita was leaving the retirement center at the end of thirty days, on September 1.

Before September arrived, Connie informed me that she could not leave her patient at Stone Village, who was dying. Barbara, the supervisor of entertainment, who Rita and I both loved, was with me and gave Connie a piece of her mind. Barbara told Connie she had made a deal with me and, she had to keep it. I just listened, for I could not get a word in between the two. Connie did say she had two other aides who could handle the job. Charlotte was one of them.

The day before Rita left the Village, I barbequed a brisket and made potato salad for the morning and night shift aides. It was a final thank you for the services they had provided Rita. Most were very reliable and had taken good care of her. Those with experience were excellent and served all the patients well. I thanked them, and many said they would miss Rita and her smiling face.

Knowing that Rita was coming home, one of my first purchases was a chair for use in the shower. Next I interviewed Charlotte, as recommended by Connie, and she turned out to be acceptable; she had the proper experience and she agreed to my hourly rate. She only wanted to work weekdays; Sundays were her church days. I told her I wanted weekend help as well. After more conversation we worked out an arrangement. I decided at that point that Connie was not reliable and could not be trusted.

To ensure that all of the aides I hired concurred with my wishes,

I made a list of things I expected them to perform each day for Rita's health. I named it, "A Day with Rita," where I listed the details of how Rita should spend her day and insisted the chart be followed. Perhaps this was something I had learned in the army and through my work as an engineer.

CHAPTER XXVIII

RITA AT HOME AGAIN

On Saturday, August 31, 2002, I drove to Stone Village, picked up Rita with her medicines and clothes, and we drove home—this time to stay. I regretted leaving Barbara and Nurse April, for they were most kind and most helpful to Rita while she was there. Rita's new caretaker, Charlotte, met us at home at one o'clock. When she arrived, Rita was in bed for her afternoon nap, and I worked at the computer while Charlotte read my rules, "A Day with Rita."

Upon Rita's awakening, Charlotte took over to become acquainted with her new patient. All went well until after dinner, when Rita had such a large BM that she had to take a shower to clean up. It was no problem; she just jumped in the shower like old times. I was surprised, for before going to Stone Village, it was very hard to get her into a shower or even a tub for a bath. I do believe she was so happy to be home again that she decided to do as we asked.

After that Rita took her medicine and went to bed with a smile on her face. I encountered a problem I hadn't expected at 2 a.m. in bed when I felt a wet brief, which required a change. It was time for another change when she got up the next morning. I wondered what I had gotten into! But I certainly did not complain. It was nice having her at home again.

Charlotte arrived after church, as we'd agreed until I had found more help. She told me that she had found someone who could work the weekends. She had asked her to come over later for an interview. It was Rose, a nurse who worked at Dauterive Hospital in New Iberia. She took over immediately for her background as a nurse in a well known hospital as well as her experience was acceptable to me. She stayed until 7:30 when Rita was put to bed. I made two more diaper changes that night. The next morning I asked the girls to try potty training Rita by sitting her on the toilet after each meal in an effort to retrain her to become more regular as well as to eliminate the changes during the night when I was on duty. It seemed to work somewhat better after a few weeks, but it was not a 100% miracle change by any means.

The following is a listing of the duties that I devised for Rita's caregivers to follow while she was at home. It was helpful for the caregivers because they understood exactly what I expected of them when they were on duty. This version of "A Day with Rita" was for her later years. It included breathing sessions that were not required during the early years. I include the schedule here as a guide for others.

RITA'S DAY
Revised 12-02-04

A.M.

8:00 A.M.   Get out of Bed, Give Breathing Treatment, Eat Breakfast and Give A.M. Medicine

9:00 A.M.   Sit on Toilet (half hour or more), Brush Teeth, Shower, Dress in different outfit each day

10:00 A.M.   Exercise, such as bending, flexing arms and legs, etc. Take Wheelchair or Golf Cart Ride (avoid LT Golf Course property). If In Wheel Chair, Stay On Sidewalk

11:00 A.M.   Break for juice and keep occupied

11:30 A.M.   Give Breathing Treatment

12:00 noon   Lunch, then sit on Toilet, Brush Teeth, and Put to Bed

SMOKING IS NOT PERMITTED OUTSIDE OR INSIDE RITA'S HOME –DON"T ASK

PM

3:00 PM   Awaken from Nap ,Dress, then give Yogurt, Juice (with thickener).

3:30 PM   Go for Walk, Read To Keep Busy, etc.

4:00 PM   Evening Shift comes on duty.

4:30 PM   Relax prior to Dinner

5:00 PM   Eat Dinner, Take Evening Medicine, then to Toilet

6:00 PM   Brush Teeth, return to living room for TV

7:30 PM   End of Day, put to Bed. Give Breathing Treatment

NOTES

1. Check every two hours for incontinence, record BMs, Walks, Wheelchair or Cart Rides
2. Maintain Nails, both hands & feet.
3. Use Lipstick & Rouge.
4. Keep Glasses Clean.
5. Need Assistance Eating Only Pureed Foods. No Straws For Liquids
6. She Will Adhere To Instructions, Most Times.

7. Check Emergency Phone Numbers AND Use When Required.
8. She likes Outdoors and Is A Good Place To Keep Her Awake.

ALWAYS KNOW LOCATION OF J. H. BOOKSH AND HOW TO REACH HIM IN AN EMERGENCY.

"A Day with Rita" was helpful to me as well as to her caregivers. There was no excuse for not following the hourly requirements. I did modify the walking exercise later due to her condition. Any outdoor activity was either in her wheelchair, riding in the golf cart, or sitting on the patio with a caregiver reading to her. Rita thoroughly enjoyed being outside in favorable weather. Later, after a suffering stroke, her exposure to the outdoors was restricted to being in the golf cart. Months later, she was to be strapped into the cart with a bottle of oxygen so she could breathe properly. Nonetheless, Rita continued to take trips out-of-doors. She enjoyed every minute she was riding and being in the fresh air.

The number and names of caregivers taking care of Rita changed with time. Charlotte did a good job finding help. Sunday was a problem day, but we were always able to have good help. It was decided that Thursday would be payday for the aides. It was no problem, since I kept the daily hours and computed what was due each caregiver. Any problem was quickly resolved.

Once while Rita was on a walk with Rose, she suddenly started running, and fell down, slightly skinning her left elbow. We were all amazed by that incident. It's strange because Rita never did any running with me. Apparently her small injury did not hurt her, as she never complained.

Because of her urinations in bed, I bought a waterproof pad in an effort to save the mattress. Incontinence is a side effect of the disease. Alzheimer's patients' brains undoubtedly revert to an early childhood mentality; the medicine cannot change their thoughts.

As Rita ate a snack in the kitchen one Saturday afternoon, Rose, her caretaker, suffered a diabetic seizure. Luckily, I was in the kitchen feeding Rita her afternoon snack when it happened. I noticed that Rose was about to fall out of her chair, so I immediately called our doctor neighbor who just happened to be at home. He came over, recognized the problem immediately, and gave her a drink of sweetened coke which revived her at once. We were lucky that the incident happened the way it did. No one was injured!

Rose was an excellent caregiver, but I could not take a chance of that happening while I was away and while she was alone with Rita. My only recourse was to release her. Later I learned that she went out for dinner the night of her seizure since this happened routinely when her sugar count was low; it wasn't anything Rose didn't expect. However, her work at the hospital was limited due to her diabetes.

I replaced Rose with Valencia, who became my best and most loyal caregiver. Valencia even replaced Charlotte later, when she had problems scheduling and recruiting additional help. Val was with me till the bitter end. When she left, I gave her a written recommendation that helped her find a job at one of the local retirement homes.

On October 3, 2002, Hurricane Lilly threatened the area. We had time to leave but decided to ride the storm out. It made landfall as a category two storm with wind gusts of seventy-five to one hundred miles per hour. It blew shingles off the roof and removed our chimney cap. We experience some minimal rain damage, but the major problem was being without electricity for several days. On the third day of being without electricity, I was determined to buy a generator. I found one, bought it, and then had to line up for gasoline. I brought it home, assembled the generator, and was about to turn it on when Val came out and said, "Thank goodness you have it going."

Actually, I had not started the generator when the lights came on. Electricity had been restored to the subdivision. I immediately called the store where I had purchased the generator and returned it without delay, since the purchase included a provision that if the electricity was restored when I got home, they would take the generator back and issue a refund. Thank goodness we had weathered another hurricane! Our local golf course was not as fortunate. Many trees were blown down, eliminating play for six days before all damage was repaired and the clean up was completed.

Anna, the new girl, came in the week after the hurricane and helped Rita exercise. They seemed to enjoy one another's company, as evidenced by my wife's constant smile. A few days later Rita celebrated her eightieth birthday. We invited two couples over for dinner to celebrate. Rita was semi-alert but very sleepy most of the time they were here.

A day later, we learned that Anna was not the person we thought she was. She was a bad housekeeper who didn't follow the guidelines. We suspected she was smoking in the bedroom, which was not allowed. My rules were no smoking inside the house. Actually, I preferred if my caretakers did not smoke, period. In any case, it was mutually agreed between Anna and me that her services were no longer required. She apologized for her mistake in judgment, but I did not like her attitude so I decided not to give her another chance.

Rita was interested and active enough to look at magazines and catalogs. Her only problem was her hemorrhoids, which we solved with Anusol salve. While she was feeling well and active, we visited Stone Village. Rita was elated to see some of her old friends and seemed to recognize the aides. Barbara, the supervisor, was most attentive to Rita who, of course, enjoyed it. Rita acted as a perfect lady, as always. It was a nice visit for her. But she did not ask to go back as a patient! I was happy having her back at home with me and would not have agreed if she had wanted to return to Stone Village.

Another of our best caretakers was Glenda, who had a regular day job but came each day for the late shift at 4:00 p.m. It was hard on her because she had a husband waiting for her at home. She stayed with us for about a year but eventually had to give in to her husband's desire. We missed her when she left.

On Friday, November 22, 2002, I celebrated my last day as a member of the Board of Directors of the Le Triomphe Homeowners' Association. Rita even celebrated with me by staying up until 9:30 p.m. I was so happy that now Rita would be my constant companion without any other interference—except maybe some occasional golf! I knew Rita was doing better overall, too, for she carefully looked at an ad for clothes at the mall! Meanwhile, we were again experimenting with Seroquel in various quantities, which helped her memory. Rita even felt well enough to go with me to vote at a local parish election on December 2, and with my help she was even able to cast her vote.

When Rita's neurologist saw her, he could see the difference in her since leaving Stone Village. He thought the change had helped her, so we made her next appointment for six months later instead of her usual three month interval. Rita was also attentive to the music she loved as a teenager and college student. We had attended a New Year's Eve party in Monroe when we lived there, and bought several of the band leaders' records. I put a few on our record player, and I'll be darned if Rita didn't keep time with the music as she did years ago. She was in her wheelchair, but we managed to dance together with her sitting down keeping time with the beat as I pulled her around the room. It was so nice to see her like that again! I enjoyed it as much as she did. We could not have won any dancing prizes, but it was so lovely to dance with her and see that famous smile of hers.

Christmas 2002 found us at home with my brother Bill and his wife, Juanita. We opened presents the night before. Rita was not too interested in opening hers, but she liked the ring and bracelet I gave her.

In February, in addition to caring for Rita, I hired painters to paint the repaired hurricane damage and the house, both inside and out. That became a problem. Every so often the painters would work for one hour or so before they disappeared. This project became a real chore, but they finally completed the job after so many months. The bathroom was not painted correctly since Rita had a BM problem when she missed the toilet, and the feces ended up on the base plates adjacent to the toilet. The new paint came off very easily when I tried to clean up Rita's mess; the base plates had not been sanded properly. The lawsuit I filed later was almost useless, since my lawyers only obtained a judgment against the painters who had cleverly had all their assets saved in their wives' names. Needless to say there were no assets to attach a judgment to so it was a useless judgment. The only person to receive any money was my lawyer friend who lived down the street from me. That is what happens when you get a jackleg to do a job when it should have been done by a certified company. My barber also heard the gory details of the transaction since he recommended the painter to me. I understand, too, that the barber was also hurt since the painter stopped having his hair cut at his shop after he raised hell with him about the job he did for me. I could have never had such a situation occur while I was working. We only dealt with reliable companies. And the old saying still goes—"You usually get what you pay for." A cheap painter does a cheap, unreliable job!!!

On February 14, 2003, a few weeks after the painters left, Rita vomited several times. Her doctor recommended a trip to the Lafayette General Hospital emergency room. We arrived at 6 p.m. and were moved to a room at midnight. The only problem the doctors could find was a packed colon. We could not understand how her colon was packed, what with her many BMs, especially after the painters left. Regardless, Rita was given a laxative, and after several days in the hospital, we came home on February 17. We were both exhausted but happy to be home again.

We made another trip to ER on March 6 after Rita could not control her shaking. A CAT scan revealed nothing, and neither did a blood test, an EKG, or x-rays. Since nothing showed up, the doctors decided it was possibly her urinary tract, which could cause a similar condition. If it had been a small stroke, they could not find any indications to show it had occurred. They concluded that she was okay, and we could return home. We did so without further delay.

Later, in discussing the problem with her doctor, who was out of town while she was in the hospital, he prescribed Rita antibiotics and Plavix, a blood thinner that she had previously taken. It seemed that her problems were now a guessing game.

Rita was fine the following month. She was her jolly, smiling self again. Several times she went out with me and friends for dinner and acted like her old self.

In late April, upon my return from playing golf, Glenda advised me that Rita had been unable to walk from the breakfast table to the bathroom for her shower so she gave her two aspirins thinking it may have been a heart attack or stroke. I asked Glenda, "Why didn't you call me from the golf course across the street when it happened?"

"I didn't think it was necessary since I gave her two aspirins in the event it was a heart attack," she responded.

"Thank heavens you did, but next time, please call me." When I saw her condition, Glenda and I immediately put her into my car and I drove to the hospital.

A CAT scan was taken, which proved nothing. They also took a sound test on her aorta artery and found no apparent blockage. The next day, a check of her throat was made to determine how she swallowed her food. After checking, the doctors suggested that Rita use a thickening agent in all liquids. Later they took an MRI and found no apparent evidence of a heart attack or blood clot. Our two doctors released her from the hospital with the provision that she stay on Plavix and take two aspirins each day. All was normal with Rita thereafter when we were at home. She walked without assistance and ate and slept well.

Two days later, Rita had a coughing spell that we could not control. I brought her back to the ER, where they removed an accumulated build up of fluid from her lungs. Rita was given another CAT scan and four x-rays of her chest. We remained in the hospital five days before returning home on Tuesday of the following week, two days later, she had another coughing spell. Back to ER we went for a quick check, but the spell cleared up while we were there, and we returned home. I needed assistance in getting her out of the car and into the house; fortunately, our gate security guard was there to help. .

Our doctor recommended that we use the services of a Home Health nurse, who could make weekly calls to assist Rita and our caregivers. One such nurse came on May 13, 2003, to explain their services, which included checking blood pressure, bathing assistance, and other nursing duties to ensure Rita was getting the best medical services at home. They also provided a hospital bed that could be raised to prevent Rita from swallowing any fluid into her lungs. She was better off in that bed because she could sleep with her head elevated between thirty and fifty degrees.

On May 21, 2003, the caregivers and I had trouble waking Rita from a deep sleep. I called Home Health; they recommended that I call 911, but before the ambulance arrived, a St. Martin Parish police deputy knocked on my door. I asked why he was there, and he said it was routine whenever someone called 911 in St. Martin Parish. The ambulance arrived, and the paramedics checked Rita and suggested she go to the hospital. We did, and once again a blood check and CAT scan revealed nothing. After discussing her condition with our doctor, he said we could return home. We did, and Rita ate a good supper. She also slept well that night. No reason was given as to why we hadn't been able to awaken her.

Two days later Rita was again coughing and trying to spit up white mucus from her mouth. Her stomach was moving violently up and down. I called 911 and received a deputy sheriff before the ambulance, which arrived at 10:15. They immediately picked her up, bed sheets and all, and we headed for the hospital, with me following closely behind them in my car. At the hospital, they tore off Rita's gown, gave her a shot, and then inserted an IV and started feeding her oxygen, followed by another CAT scan. They found nothing. We were assigned a room and remained in the hospital four more days. The doctors could not decide if her latest problem was a seizure or what, but they finally let us return home.

When I write that Rita and I went to the hospital, I do mean that I was always with her day and night. I did return home after several days for a few hours to shower and change clothes. I slept on the couch in the hospital room adjacent to Rita, who knew I was with her the entire stay. We often held hands so as to reassure her I was there. The couch was not a comfortable bed, but I could not leave her alone, and I know she did not want to stay in a hospital alone. I felt I could sleep later at home. I often wondered what would have happened to her had she been at Stone Village with this recent bout of problems. Would Stone Village have gotten her medical attention as fast as I did?

When we returned home from the latest hospital stay, Home Health sent over a lung treatment machine for the removal of mucus from her throat. I also employed a speech therapist in an attempt to revive Rita's speech, which she had lost several times after her recent trips to the hospital. The female therapist said, after one examination, she did not believe Rita would ever speak again. I suggested that she should not think that way so soon. One attempt did not satisfy me. We then had a second speech nurse come in to examine Rita, who showed more interest and believed she could be taught to speak again.

Meanwhile, Rita went back to seeming like her old self again, but she did not speak. She was not sleeping very well at night until we changed her breathing treatments to late afternoon instead of at bedtime. She slept much better after the change. We also got her to walk, with and without assistance.

About this time, a second therapist came to assist Rita in her walking. She was given exercises to try to strengthen her legs and arms. It seemed to help her, for I was then able to help her unassisted to get into the car for rides around town. She was eating well then but seemed to tire easily from the exercise.

A request from Home Health was that I remove the door and the plastic enclosure from around the shower, replacing them with a curtain. She believed it would make it easier to guide Rita into the shower and seat her in the shower chair. I did remove most of what they wanted but refused to remove the nine-inch step between the shower and the bath floor. To remove it would have required a drain in the bathroom floor, which I felt could be avoided with a little imagination. Everything worked okay without the step's removal. Home Health's aide and our private caregivers had no problems getting Rita into and out of the shower without injury.

Following the episodes in the hospital, Rita and I visited her neurologist who believed the recent problems were the result of a stroke. Because her right eye was partially closed, and her left hand and ankle were swollen, the doctor thought she had suffered a stroke. He agreed we needed the services of a speech therapist to improve or correct Rita's speech. He prescribed Protonix for her stomach. He believed that too much Seroquel affected Rita's her sleeping pattern, so he also reduced her dosage. Finally, he reaffirmed the need for a wheelchair and explained that he thought Rita would not die from her present condition; some other disease, such as pneumonia, he reasoned, would be more likely cause her death.

The new speech therapist believed she could indeed help Rita with her speech. She would try her best. That was all we asked. Rita's walking therapist also came and had her walking about fifty wobbly feet at a stretch. It was some progress, but not great! Rita was very good with Sandra, one of the new caretakers and was eventually strong enough to go downtown to have her glasses adjusted.

Later on that day the frown on her face told me something wasn't right. I asked, "What is wrong with you? Do you want to sit in your chair?"

She answered quickly, "Yeah!" It was great to hear her speak again. I had begun to notice that she did not always understand words and questions when we spoke to her. We were elated at her progress. Once again, she was smiling after getting into "her chair." After this, some days she spoke all day; other days she was quiet and did not have anything to say. She did have an interest in one of her favorite TV programs, *The Lawrence Welk Show*, which we watch every Saturday night.

Between speech therapists, exercise therapists, and Home Health aides for showers, we entertained Rita to keep her busy. She was taken for wheelchair rides around the neighborhood and car trips to stores where we usually pushed her around in her wheelchair. She seemed interested in the sights wherever we took her. We did have trouble at times with her wheezing and coughing.

One night in early April 2003, I attempted to remove an accumulation of mucus from her stomach, but it got so bad that I called 911 for an ambulance. The medical technicians decided that Rita needed more care in a hospital, so off they went with Rita in the ambulance and me following closely behind. We arrived at 9:45. First they gave her a breathing exercise, and then they drained her lung mucus with a tube through her nose and took a chest x-ray of her lungs.

The next morning Rita had another test of her swallowing. It was decided that aspiration was causing the trouble, but she was able to swallow very well. Finally on July 11, we were allowed to leave the hospital. It seemed the mucus that had built up in her lungs caused the trouble. We tried smaller meals in small portions, which seemed to work for a while. Rita was then given four breathing exercises every day to keep her lungs clear.

We made an appointment with another doctor on August 26 to find out why she continued with the aspirations. After the examination, he told us that Rita's esophagus and stomach had no obstructions that would cause aspirations. He believed that if the food reached her esophagus, it should go into her stomach since there were no restrictions to stop the entry. We left with no immediate answer or solution, just more questions regarding her problems!

Then, on September 9 Rita started wheezing after taking her

medicine. We tried suction, but it did not help. Matters got worse, so I called 911. The ambulance arrived and off to the hospital we went. Lafayette General was overcrowded, so we detoured to Our Lady of Lourdes Hospital, arriving at 9 p.m. The physicians concluded that the medicine, Benzonatte, that Rita had chewed, instead of swallowed, had caused the trouble. This I doubted. Later results of an x-ray of Rita's lungs showed that she had a small case of pneumonia.

The next day the doctor questioned the diagnosis because they had no x-rays to compare it to. I wondered what had happened to all those taken at Lafayette General, but we were in a different hospital. Rita had a fever and was taking antibiotics. Because no other prognosis was made, we were released from the hospital and arrived at home in the late afternoon, just before supper. Rita was much better, in good spirits, and very alert.

It was around this time that the problems with Charlotte began. She was picky about everything and threatened to leave. She commented, "I thought I was in charge, but I am only being paid the same as others."

"I was considering raising your hourly rate by fifty cents an hour, but you want a dollar more," I answered.

This went on for some time before she calmed down. She liked Rita and wanted to care for her, and she did not want to leave. I agreed paying her the extra dollar an hour starting that day.

Rita perked up after a few days when her antibiotics cycle was completed. But then her hemorrhoids were worsening. A new medicine helped. So after, she was her smiling self, talking as always. Back in good shape! Her doctor took her off both the Premarin and Prozac.

I was beginning to notice bruises on Rita's arms, legs, and other parts of her body. I believe it was poor handling by a single caregiver. I suggested that, when possible, that caregiver have someone else assist her if others were in the house. If it was not an emergency, the person was asked to wait until I was around. I tried to make clear the fact that they were handling very valuable property of mine; I did not care for bruises. Rita was my most valuable asset! My request helped somewhat.

For the past few months Rita had been sleeping in a hospital bed in our bedroom while I was in our king-size bed adjacent to her. Her side of my bed was unused, and I believe Rita was tired of the small hospital bed. One night after seeming downcast all day, I asked, "Would you like to get out of that bed and sleep with me in your bed?"

Without a yes or no, she almost jumped out of bed, and with my help, we walked the few feet to her side of the king-size bed without any problem. I do not believe either she or I had a good night's sleep being together again in the same bed, but it only took a few nights for her to get reacquainted with her old bed, and we were able to sleep like old times. I had the local rental company pick up the hospital bed because Rita was again with me in her bed and apparently not suffering from mucus accumulation.

Rita celebrated her eighty-first birthday on October 19 with a cocktail (without the booze) and watched me grill a steak on the patio, like old times. I actually believed she knew that it was her birthday. She was happy, gay, and smiling throughout the day. Her former caretaker nurse, Lisa, called to wish her a happy birthday and tell us she was now working at a doctor's office. I believed we should have had more birthday parties for Rita after watching the change and excitement I saw in her.

I read that a new medicine for dementia, Memantine, was about to become available in the States in January 2004. I immediately asked our doctor about the possibility of getting a supply before 2004. He said if I could locate a source before then, it was agreeable with him to purchase it. On the Internet I found a supply in London. It was a new European drug helping dementia patients. When it arrived, Rita was given varying amounts until the doctor thought it was adequate. I remember that the drug made Rita very sleepy, but she was able to eat properly and was more herself than before. We thought it was a lifesaver.

Christmas 2003 found us at home alone, for the most part. I smoked a turkey and had my nephew, John D., and his mother over for dinner. Val, the caretaker, arrived with a cold, so I asked that she wash her hands many times during the day and not touch Rita. I did not want Rita to catch a cold in her condition.

The next day, Rita felt so well that she assisted me in cooking supper. The month of January found her in fairly good shape but still in the need of breathing exercises. Her doctor gave her pills that helped her sleep more during the night. We celebrated our fifty-seventh wedding anniversary on February 4. That day, she walked into kitchen to talk with me while I was fixing dinner. Charlotte had been trying to teach her to play cards, but she was not interested. Later in the month, I had a dinner party for several friends, which Rita attended with the rest of us. She acted very well but was sleepy.

I did take a day off of caring for Rita when a friend in Monroe died. I drove there to attend the memorial service for Art, a friend and golfing buddy Rita and I met when we lived there. He had dementia, and he had fallen and died as a result of the fall. While I was gone, Charlotte said Rita was fine.

Rita suffered a mishap on February 25. When Charlotte returned from the kitchen with a drink for Rita, she found her out like a light, sitting in her wheelchair. She called me. Rita was limp for ten to fifteen minutes before Charlotte was able to revive her using a wet towel. I gave Rita an aspirin, fearing it may have been a stroke. It must have been a seizure instead because she recovered enough to eat supper shortly thereafter and slept all night in bed. She recovered quickly and spoke very well, as if nothing had happened. The next day, as I put drops in her nose to clear it up, she said, "Thank you."

March 16, 2004, was our parting of ways with Charlotte. She had been hard on Val and was treating her like a yoyo, changing work days to favor her and her friends. She said people were talking behind her back about the many changes she made with the caregivers. I asked if I was the one. She said no but thought it best if she left Rita regardless of how she loved her and enjoyed taking care of her. I told her she did a good job with Rita, but I could not stand the constant bickering of the caregivers. I paid her off, and she left that day. I did not hear from her again until Rita's death, when she called to express her condolences.

Val took over as was my number-one caregiver, and she did an excellent job. We needed additional help, but when I asked her about her sister, she did not want to tell me anything about her. She did bring in her cousin Gail, who worked the afternoon shift. Gail was okay and Rita liked her.

Rita and Sandra, the weekend caregiver, and I were able to go out for a shrimp and crawfish dinner. Rita enjoyed the shrimp while we ate boiled crawfish. The following week we took Rita in the golf cart to our golf course to watch the professional golf tournament. She was not too excited but silently watched the players play the game she formerly enjoyed so much.

Val only had one accident with Rita. After returning from a wheelchair ride one day, she took Rita out of the wheelchair, put her in her favorite chair in the living room, and went into the kitchen to obtain a drink for her when Val heard a thud! She rushed into the living room, where she found that Rita had fallen from the chair and hit her head on the adjacent end table. She had damaged her cheek and suffered a cut above her right eye. It was a minor cut, only about an inch long. I came in about that time and soon reported the mishap to her doctor, who suggested I take her to the ER at the nearest hospital. We did. Stitches were not necessary; she was given only a bandage of glue to help the wound close, a tetanus shot, and several antibiotic pills. The cut healed within a week and left no scar. It was strange how so many other bruises occurred, and no one knew how they happened. At least we were sure of this one.

Perhaps I should have had cameras in each room to capture and verify each accident. Sometimes it may have been Rita's fault, but I became suspicious of those aides who always had no idea how the bruises occurred. In any case, after this incident, I required a new order immediately, which read: "Never leave Rita in a wheelchair without the safety belt buckled across her knees!"

By Easter, Rita was becoming herself again and was eating well after a spell of just picking at her food. Later in the month when Bill and Juanita visited us, we, all went out to a nearby seafood restaurant for dinner. Rita ordered her favorite, boiled crabs. She enjoyed them after we helped in the peeling.

The next day, we loaded her wheelchair and drove to Morgan City to attend the unveiling of a wall painting of the John R. Drackett, a ferryboat my grandfather formerly owned and operated for automobiles between Berwick and Morgan City. The ferry was in operation prior to construction of the Huey P. Long Bridge across the Atchafalaya River. The painting, on the wall of a downtown building, was an exact replica of the original boat as I remembered it. My mother often spoke of collecting fees on it as a teenager. I also remembered how we kids always watched Grandpa count the daily receipts on his dining room table. At times he would throw a few nickels and dimes to us as he counted. We were amazed and thankful.

Rita was not too interested in listening to the long-winded politicians at the unveiling and easily fell asleep in her wheelchair. We and others in attendance would have done the same if we had a chair to sit on. Regardless, we enjoyed the presentation and the tribute given to our grandfather.

On our return home, we had to buy a new suction tube because Rita was coughing and spitting up small amounts of mucus. It seemed that she was like the weather. When it was cloudy and rainy, she was the same way, not too bright and sunny. After a good night's sleep, she was okay again—talking, walking, and smiling at everyone. Rita continued to have her good and bad days; the constant changes in help affected her daily routine.

Val was my most reliable caretaker now, but we had a number of replacement caregivers who made it harder on Val and me. On August 1, 2004, we had another scare that prompted me to call 911. Rita was in bed after lunch. She was limp and seemed to have trouble breathing. Our neighbor doctor across the street checked her pulse and said it was very low. By the time the ambulance arrived, Rita was wide awake, and her vitals were all normal, according to the ambulance technician. He said he thought Rita was okay, but if I wanted, they would take her to the hospital. I said no; she was normal the rest of the day. She talked a lot, ate lunch and dinner, and then slept just fine all night. I was the one who couldn't sleep because of my hay fever, but I caught up the next night.

The following day we visited Rita's doctor, who said she was in good shape and made the next appointment for three months in the future. After the visit, the three of us had lunch at the club. Rita ordered a large shrimp salad, ate some, and then finished it at supper.

Several nights later another good friend, Etta Mae, died of an asthma attack. She and Horace, my boyhood friend, had visited us everywhere we had lived in the States (but not Australia). Horace had met Etta Mae after the war. I knew that life without her would be hard on him. He would be alone, since they had no children, just like Rita and me. I dreaded to think how I would feel if Rita left me suddenly. I attended Etta Mae's funeral and promised to see Horace often. I did until he died suddenly in 2007.

In September 2004 I called the doctor because Rita was having trouble breathing and her nose was stopped up. He sent antibiotics for a respiratory condition, which helped immediately. After several days, Rita was able to go for a ride and was very alert and talkative as normal.

September 12 found Rita almost fainted on the toilet. The caregiver on duty put her to bed. When I saw her, she was very pale and cool to touch. I called for an ambulance, and we arrived at the hospital about 7 p.m. It was decided there were some problems with her heart, but the main problem was her aspiration of fluid into the lungs. We were in the hospital for five days, until the afternoon of September 17, when her lungs were finally cleared. Several days later, Rita was okay and ready for a haircut.

To enter the barbershop, customers had four steps to step up before reaching the main floor. In the past Rita and had I struggled once or twice up the stairs before Brock, one of the weight-lifting young barbers, would meet us at the car, pick Rita up—all hundred and fifteen pounds—then carry her up the four steps and put her in Kenny's chair. After the haircut, Brock would again pick her up, walk down the steps with her in his arms, and seat her in the backseat of the car. What a strong young man he was, and still is today! He always refused a tip, which I attempted to give him several times. He said it was his contribution to Rita. I shall never forget Brock and Kenny and how they catered to Rita. They were so accommodating.

About this time we had begun to wonder about our regular doctor and the "quick examinations" he gave Rita when we saw him. He was nice, cordial, and well- respected in Lafayette but seemed to just take Rita's blood pressure, listen to her heart, and say, "Come back in three months." We liked his hospital manner, for when he was out of town his two partners were available to see Rita when we went to the hospital. He had been our doctor since we moved back to Louisiana— more than fifteen years. The main reason we finally changed, however, was a friend's recommendation of a doctor who gave shots for sinus problems, which Rita and I both suffered and needed. Our doctor only gave medicines.

On September 23 the new doctor found Rita's lungs still had fluid and recommended a chest x-ray and blood test at a local clinic. He also prescribed an antibiotic. At home the next day, a caregiver, Loretta, was with Rita when I walked in after lunch and found both asleep. Loretta had been with us only a few days and had already screwed up on several things she was supposed to do for Rita. I believed Rita did not like her because her attitude changed each day Loretta was around. Rita always became more alert when Val was with her. Loretta had given Rita a dress for reasons unknown, which I returned to her, together with her bottled water she brought with her and a check for the time she sat with Rita. I did not tolerate sleeping on the job. Before she left, she apologized for not performing her job to our expectations, but I could not stand her or anyone ignoring Rita by sleeping.

Results from a later chest x-ray of Rita's proved negative, and the doctor believed she should drink more water, get more exercise, and breathe deeply to get her lungs to function more efficiently. He also prescribed an antihistamine, Zyrtec, and thought Rita's oxygen level should be measured and recorded. To obtain her oxygen level, a device was strapped to her finger. The exam was supposed to last the entire night, but Rita lasted only six hours before she pulled the meter off. As far as exercise, Rita was only able to ride in my golf cart. It was hard for her to walk very far.

Another scare occurred on October 9 when Rita was getting a breathing treatment. She rebelled against the treatment; her face was a deep red, and she had begun to perspire profusely. Since we had taken flu shots the day before, I thought it was a normal reaction. I called an ambulance any way, and my suspicion was confirmed. Even the technicians thought Rita was rebellious about taking the breathing treatments. There was no fluid in her lungs. After the ambulance left, she went to sleep and slept soundly until the next morning.

We had a new caregiver the next day when Val's sister came to work. We found later that we were now at the bottom of the barrel regarding caregivers. As days went on, we learned the sister was not at all like Val. With that in mind, I did give her several chances.

Rita celebrated her eighty-second birthday on October 19. She had ice cream and cake with several of our friends who came over to celebrate the day with us. Later that afternoon, it was hard for her to breathe. After receiving one of her Zyrtec pills, she was able to eat her snacks in the kitchen, and at dinner also she ate well. She was in bed at 7:20 p.m. when Clara, our second-shift caretaker, started to give her a breathing treatment. She began sweating and had a difficult time breathing. The caretaker suggested I call an ambulance, which I did. It arrived in twenty-five minutes. They tried to give her an IV but could not get a needle into her right hand. We then rushed to Lourdes Hospital, since our new doctor preferred it to Lafayette General. When we arrived in the ER, the staff immediately put Rita on oxygen and treated her for congestive heart failure. They believed her heart was not pumping enough oxygen to clear the lungs of accumulated liquids. After an x-ray, this was found not to be the case. There was no fluid in her lungs. The oxygen flow was continued, and she slept well.

During her stay in the hospital, Rita had another swallowing test. Also, a specialist in pulmonary diseases informed us that if one had smoked even a short time and stopped, that person would have defective lungs. (Rita had smoked a few years in high school but had stopped when I met her in 1946. It had been about ten or eleven years since had she smoked.) He also discussed life support for Rita. I inquired, if it was necessary and if she was revived from a stopped heartbeat, would she be able to live a regular life thereafter? He said yes and gave some examples of those brought back to life. He also advised that Rita could not live on Cortisone, which she was then on.

That afternoon as we were talking about this Rita's condition, a nurse came in to alert us that Rita's heartbeat had slowed to forty beats a minute. She was revived, and then she slept. Her blood pressure had fallen to 160/40. Rita was fine thereafter. We were allowed to return home on the twenty-fifth.

Rita was then put on oxygen full-time at home. She did not necessarily like it, but she became accustomed to it. When she rode in the golf cart, a bottle of oxygen went with her. It may have been troublesome, but it kept her alive, which was my motive. Meanwhile, I was hoping for a miracle.

No miracle came. On November 2, 2004, Rita fell asleep in a chair and could not be awakened for lunch. I called an ambulance. She was taken to the hospital with a blood pressure reading of 108/50. There was a little rattle in her lungs. Another CAT scan at the hospital revealed mucus accumulation. We were released after two nights in the hospital, and Rita was okay after the few days.

The only change was that the new doctor wanted Rita to check her sleeping habits with an overnight apnea test. So off we went to the apnea clinic, which seemed to be the fad at the time. Rita slept very little there, for I was next to her in bed. We returned home at about 5:00 the next morning. It was a waste of time; we had to do it over because the records were incomplete. Then it turned out to be a double waste of time, as they prescribed a mask that Rita used only a few days. She begged me to take it off her each night, and finally after three days I decided she had enough other problems and removed it. The poor girl had enough to bother her besides a mask. I know, for I tried one later and swore that I, too, would not be able to wear one to sleep.

Rita was constantly having medical visitors: Home Health for baths and examinations, a walking therapist, and her two caregivers. On November 12 I had to call 911 again after starting her daily breathing treatment. She had turned red again and was perspiring heavily. When the ambulance arrived, her breathing had improved, and her vitals were normal. I decided to keep her at home. Later she was okay and able to eat supper. The following day, she went to town with me to have her hair cut.

Thanksgiving was a few days later. We ate alone and let Val have dinner with her family. Rita was no trouble with me. Our neighbors down the street provided an extra meal, for I had already cooked a Thanksgiving dinner.

On Sunday, December 12, Val's sister was on duty. She took Rita for a cart ride and came back with a plate of barbecue. I asked where she got it, and she said at the club. I exploded, "Didn't you know you were not to take Rita in a cart or wheelchair anywhere on country club property? It's too dangerous, and they asked me that she not be exposed to the danger, with so many club carts running around."

"I didn't know I wasn't allowed on the property," was her response.

"Didn't you read the 'A Day with Rita' listing? That was definitely included," I said, showing her the rules.

With that she said, "If you will make out my check, I will leave. Nobody has ever talked to me that way."

I promptly did make out her check, and when I gave it to her, she said, "You don't like the color of my skin."

I said, "I don't care what color your skin is. It could be green, yellow, white, or whatever. As I said, I do not want Rita brought on club property, and I have been asked by club officials not to let anyone bring her in my cart on the club grounds."

She mumbled something about how I should be paying overtime for weekend work, and with that I opened the front door and let her out. It was good riddance; I never should have hired her. That night she called to apologize, saying she was not brought up the way she had behaved and asked if she could return next Saturday. I said, "If you conform to my rules, okay." She agreed but did not return.

We tried a new breathing mask for Rita on Thursday of the following week for her afternoon nap. It helped her sleep until her 3:30 wake-up time. As she and I were eating a cookie in the kitchen later, the doorbell rang, and I was surprised to see a young lady at the door; she had not been announced by the security gate. I assumed she was a nurse from Health Care and let her in. She wanted to see Rita, so I brought her into the kitchen. I asked when they had changed nurses at Home Health because the lady was not familiar to me.

She informed me that she was from social services and had been asked by an unnamed source to check Rita for bruises. I informed her, "Only nurses and doctors that I know check my wife. If you get an okay from them, I might let you check her. Otherwise, you need to leave my home immediately."

I escorted her to the door. I could not believe anyone would do such a thing. I also called the gate and asked the guard why he had let this girl in unannounced. He told me she had flashed a badge and said she did not want to be announced. I explained that our rule was to call a resident before letting in anyone who was not listed on a permitted entry list for that address.

The next day, the Home Health aide came to bathe Rita, and she told me that the social worker had called them, and she had read the riot act to her, explaining that I had never caused any bruises on Rita. If she had any, they were all accidental.

Rita awoke after her nap. The new sleeping mask left a ring around her eye. It must not have fitted correctly around her face and rubbed against her eye. Regardless of the benefit, I decided against the new mask and sent it back. Rita was happy about my decision.

That night I received a call from a male claiming he was a doctor calling in reference to an investigation being conducted by the state social services department concerning examining my wife for bruises. I suspected it wasn't a real doctor, for doctors don't always make calls; their nurses usually do. In addition, I recognized an accent, far different from a southern Louisiana accent, and I knew it was not a doctor. I immediately called the sheriff's office in St. Martin Parish to file a complaint and to possibly make an arrest of the man I suspected was causing the problem—I thought strongly that it was Val's sister and her boyfriend bothering me. The sheriff suggested I obtain a caller identification box from the telephone company to document the number from which the call was made. With that information, I could press charges after an investigation was completed. The next day I purchased the box, but I never received another call from the individuals. Go figure!

Our doctor's nurse, someone who knew the offender, commented, "I can't understand how you ever hired her to take care of Mrs. Booksh. I wouldn't let that individual care for my dog! I will call the state and straighten this out once and for all."

She did, and the case was closed. The individual in question never set foot in my house again. I did keep her sister, who was an excellent caregiver.

Christmas 2004 was Rita and my last Christmas together. Val came over in the morning to bathe Rita, and we were alone the rest of the day. Rita again was not too enthused about Christmas when opening her packages. But with my help, she opened them all. Maybe it was not exactly as it was in the old days, but Rita appeared happy with her gifts. It was also nice being alone with her, like old times when we lived away from Louisiana.

In my notes of the day, I wrote that I doubted Rita's dementia was real because she was so knowledgeable and knew what tube to pull out of her nose when she chose to dislike a certain procedure. She was then on oxygen twenty-four hours a day but, like a baby, she did not realize the need for it. With oxygen, she was able to breathe easier, and it prolonged her life.

We spent New Year's Day alone after Val gave Rita a shower. Val went home soon after putting Rita to bed because she was not feeling well; she promised that she would see a doctor immediately. Val's illness kept her away for several days, so Clara helped me in the meantime. Home Health also provided services for several days.

I took Rita to our new doctor during this time, and he was amazed at how well she looked. Her blood pressure was good at 130/70. She was well enough for a trip to Abbeville, a small town 20 miles south of Lafayette noted for oysters and other seafood. Rita ate very little, and slept during the half an hour drive home.

We had gone to the doctor on Tuesday, and by Saturday I had to call an ambulance. The substitute caregiver from Home Health had, when giving Rita a breathing treatment, held the mask too tightly around her nose and caused her to perspire profusely. Even her hair was wet.

Again we were off to the hospital. We arrived at Lourdes Hospital at 8:20 p.m. The ER doctors found that she had aspirated, and there was evidence of pneumonia in her left lung. She had been given a breathing treatment in the ambulance and again at the hospital. At midnight we were finally moved into room 315. Our doctor was out of town, but his PA assistant, Jason, contacted him, and he agreed she should be in the hospital, so we remained there for treatment.

Our doctor arrived the next day and suggested a tube be inserted in Rita's stomach for feeding. He believed it was the only salvation for the aspiration. I asked if feeding her food the consistency of honey one more time would help before inserting a tube. He repeated his recommendation. Then he wondered about Rita's consent. I told him that Rita had agreed to a tube for her mother under the same circumstances and therefore would not object if one was absolutely required. He returned with, "I believe she could live that way until pneumonia takes her life later." (Thanks, I said to myself!. What a satisfying remark to tell her husband, who would have done anything to keep her alive!)

I called Rita's neurologist who we had been going to for years and who knew her condition better than most. He came over, and we discussed her condition. He said that she was at the end of the eight-year cycle that Alzheimer's often displayed. He advised against putting a tube in her stomach. He suggested that I take her home and let nature take its course. He explained that she might live to Christmas, but was doubtful that she would live to July. He knew I did not want to let her go, but he and I had been truthful with one another throughout the years. He had helped me through many questionable hours, and I felt that I could talk with him anytime he was available.

Another doctor was called in to check for any blockage in Rita's throat and found none. He believed food and mucus were causing all the problems. Our doctor came in to talk to about me discussing Rita's case with hospice after I had inquired about their services. He was against hospice. "They will only take her off all medicines then send her home to die," he protested.

He still believed a stomach tube was Rita's only salvation. I agreed and asked him to call a surgeon in and do it immediately, but Rita had to get better first. A cardiologist was called in for an examination of her heart.

On January 13, 2005, Rita was still hanging on. Our doctor was convinced that the tube in her stomach was the only solution. He also suggested I not revive her in the event of a heart attack, which was possible. I talked to hospice and listened to their suggestions. They wanted me to sign an agreement with them, but I hesitated, for at the time I did not want to see Rita die. The surgeon said he would insert a tube into her stomach but had to wait until the wheezing stopped, perhaps within a week. I asked how the operation was done, and he gave me the gory details. Another doctor said that he thought, after hearing all the possibilities, I had made the correct decision. One can always call hospice later. On the night of January 14, I slept at home since I had Cathy available to stay with Rita.

In the morning of the fifteenth, I returned to the hospital and spent the day with Rita before leaving to sleep at home because Cathy was to be with her again. Rita's breathing was labored, and her left hand was swollen. The same routine was followed during the sixteenth, when Val stayed with Rita that night, and I slept at home after being with her all day. The next morning when I arrived, January 18, 2005, a day before my birthday, I noticed that Rita's breathing was extremely labored, and she acted as though she was gasping for air. I asked Val if the doctor had been there earlier. She said no, only Jason, the PA. I asked what they were doing about the way Rita was gasping for breath. I was told that Rita's doctor had been contacted and was coming over to see her soon.

I was tempted then to call the nurse but decided to wait for the doctor. A half an hour later, I noticed that Rita had stopped breathing and called the nurse's station. It so happened that the doctor who handled the resuscitation unit was at the desk. He rushed into the room. I pleaded, "Please do everything possible to bring her back to life." I didn't care what the chart said. I wanted her alive. I wanted her breathing again.

"Please wait in the hall," he ordered.

They worked on her for a few minutes then came out of her room and said, "Nothing more can be done."

My beloved wife Rita was gone after almost fifty-eight years of married life. She died on January 18, 2005, one day before my birthday. Actually we were together more than fifty-eight years counting our courtship year. Marriage was heaven on earth with her. Now she was gone, and I felt so guilty for not calling for help earlier. Could she have been saved? I will never know. After a few minutes, our doctor called to offer his condolences. "I am so sorry," he said.

While I did not agree with all he did, he at least acknowledged one thing: that was that I should have asked why he hadn't been there with me, but it was too late. Rita's suffering was over, and I was alone—alone after all those beautiful years together. She will live forever in my memory, for I have lived my life in heaven. I cannot imagine a life more heavenly than the one I had with Rita. How lucky I have been!

Rita was buried in Lafayette Memorial Park Cemetery in one

of the two lots we purchased over twenty years prior from my good friend Al. He had no use for them since he was remarried, and his new wife had other arrangements. The wake was held at Delhomme Funeral Home. Her many friends and kin paid their last respects to her. A Dutch Catholic priest who had a terrible accent conducted her funeral service because Rita had drifted away from her regular Catholic church services and had no regular priest. To us, that meant nothing because we had lived a wonderful life together; one in which we were proud of, and one that exemplified the Catholic religion as well as my Episcopal faith.

Now I visit her grave weekly and discuss my new life with her during each visit. I know I will be with her one of these days, since my burial plot is located right beside hers. I do have something to look forward to—to sleep with her once again and to continue our lives together in heaven as we lived so many years on earth.

CHAPTER XXIX

My Life Alone

Living alone is not as enjoyable as having a loved one with you each and every day. I was on the go most of the time during Rita's and my over fifty-seven plus years of married life. At times we were separated while I was working out of town; however, we had many years together sandwiched between my travels. When I retired in 1984, at sixty-two years of age, we were together every day until January 2005, for almost twenty-one years. While Rita's last ten years could not compare to her good or normal years before dementia entered our daily lives, we were at least able to hold and be with one another. She lived with dementia for almost ten years, but I honestly believe she knew who I was, her lover, until the day she died. I know I loved her from the first day I met her after World War II.

After that fatal day in January 2005, I purposely arranged the house and pictures such that I will not forget her. Her image is strategically located in the bedroom, my office, the living room, and the hall along with other pictures. My brain and heart are other places where her image will never be replaced. There will never be another like my beloved Rita. Many have asked why I have not remarried. What a silly question: How can I? Rita is still my wife! She may be gone physically, but she is now in heaven waiting for me to join her.

I was reminded of her a year after her death when it was necessary that I spend almost two weeks in the hospital with MRSA, or Methicillin-resistant *Staphylococcus Aureus*. The disease is usually contracted through shared items or surfaces that have come in contact with someone else's infection (such as dirty towels, used bandages, and other items in a hospital). Perhaps I did not practice good personal hygiene when I was in and out of so many hospitals during Rita's illness. But I do now!

Once I asked a nurse, "Why don't you wear a mask when you attend to me like the others do?"

She said, "I don't have to if I wash regularly. Further, half the people walking in the streets today have MRSA and don't even know it!"

It was a painless hospital stay, but at the time, I would have rather been at home since I was in the midst of negotiating a fee for an oil and gas lease on land our family owns. A hospital is not an appropriate place to discuss a financial arrangement. I also learned that my doctor was on vacation, and so I only had contact with the nurses. I finally called the doctor's office and requested another doctor to discuss my case with me. That was better than not having any doctor.

Finally the doctor returned, but he would not discuss any further about my going home. I believed I could have as easily taken the medicine at home. When I insisted that I be immediately discharged from the hospital, he finally agreed. Then he gave me a prescription for ten more pills than Medicare would not pay for since I was then a home patient, and medicine is only paid while in a hospital. It was worth the six-hundred dollars I paid for the pills. I also kissed that doctor good-bye for good; he was the one who had not helped Rita in her last days, and he certainly had not helped me. The parting was mutual and a relief! Now I have a new, more understanding doctor. I still regret doing business with that doctor who was treating Rita when she died.

In March 2006 I was hospitalized for a carotid artery operation. It was on the left side of my throat and proved to be only an overnight hospital stay. I was able to play golf a week later. Since then, I have avoided all hospitals. Rita and I spent enough time there to last me a lifetime.

Since then, my days have been centered around golf, much as it was for most of my retirement life. If I don't play three or four rounds per week, I feel as though I am wasting my time doing other things.

Writing this memoir has been a lifesaver. I don't mind missing golf when I am writing about Rita. While she was with me, I enjoyed doing things for her. Cooking for her was one of those things. Now it seems I have lost my knack for it. I still cook, but my food is not as tasty as it once was. Eating alone never was one of my favorite pastimes, and it has not changed.

I still do my own shopping, but not as religiously as I did on Mondays when Rita was alive. There are several reasons for my attitude change: First, I don't need as much food as when I was feeding the two of us. Secondly, the freezer is overstocked now. And finally, I eat less now than before. When my friend Horace was alive, we usually had lunch together on Thursdays, my rest day from golf. Now that he has left this earth, my Thursdays are free, but if the weather is a respectful eighty degrees, I may play golf instead. The summers are just too warm in southern Louisiana for very much golf in July and August. I'll leave the high nineties and hundred degree temperatures for the youngsters. Air conditioning and writing are far more comfortable.

Eating in southern Louisiana can get one too heavy for the scales. Our gumbos, étoufées, fried shrimp and crawfish, and so on, are heavy in calories. We try, on occasion, to skip such heavy meals. Meat is very good here, but red meat, I am told, is not good for you. It seems we all prefer meals that taste good but are high in calories and cholesterol. Gravies don't help the waistline either.

Exercise, I know, can help reduce the waist line. Early in 2007 and the latter part of the previous year, I began exercising regularly at the club until I hurt my back on the golf course. My sciatic nerve had acted up for the third year in a row causing pain on my right side buttock and thigh. The therapist, who lives in LeTriomphe, had treated the last two attacks, but I thought the new exercise room at the club would cure or stabilize it this time. A very muscular trainer tried to treat it with exercise but with little success, but it became more painful. I quit the exercise plan and went back to my therapist who, within three weeks, had me back on the golf course. Now I exercise at home with some success. This year I have had no problems!

Being alone in the house had me reading magazines and books that Rita had accumulated over the years. One day while I was reading, I came across an advertisement that listed the many dangers of living alone after retirement. I succumbed to the advertisement and enlisted the aid of an "on-call system" from California. I could, by pressing a button, call the services of a local ambulance, if required. After a year, I changed to a local ambulance service which offered a lower monthly rate with the hope I will never need the service. I do recommend such a service for any retiree who is living alone. If needed, in an emergency, I only have to press a button for ambulance service.

Another safekeeping idea I thought of was to give a neighbor a key to my house to check on me occasionally. Sometimes it is days between times when I venture out. My friend Horace was found in a pool of blood by his neighbors one morning when he had not opened a shade in his kitchen window, a daily routine. The neighbors had a key to his home and found him having fallen and hit his head on a nightstand the night before. He died ten days later in the hospital. Had he subscribed to an "on call" ambulance service, perhaps he may have been able save his life by pushing a button to call an ambulance. Regardless, neighbors with a house key may also be of some assistance in an emergency.

I live two miles from the nearest grocery and drug store. I formerly shopped in Lafayette about fifteen miles away, but the older I get, the more I shop nearby. The gasoline crunch in mid 2008 also had something to do with it. However, I am physically able, at age eighty-seven, to drive and am in good health. My eyes, thank goodness, are correctable to 20/20, and bifocals handle my distant problems. My doctor compares me to a sixty-five-year-old, and I hope my health and his diagnosis are correct, for I dread the thought of living my remaining years in a retirement home. Only time will tell.

My neighbors are very thoughtful of my welfare. Even with her diabetes, Gale, who is an excellent cook, sends over delicious meals now and then. My cooking is awful compared to hers, and despite her illness, she has not forgotten how to cook those wonderful southern Louisiana goodies. Another neighbor has my key and alarm system code. When I don't show up for golf or pick up my newspaper, he usually comes over to see if I am all right. Now I am back to cutting my grass and trimming the shrubs, which may help neighbors know I am still alive.

At night I am either on the computer, reading, or watching TV. Since Rita's death, I have read over thirty novels. I am also getting to be a nut on Sudoku solving, which gets harder as the week progresses. I fail more than I succeed, but if using one's brain will prevent dementia, I will be okay in that respect..

I do not play golf on Mondays because the course is closed. To fill the time, I have joined a senior writing class to improve my writing skills. It is a small class of twelve men and women fifty years or older. We have an excellent teacher who has helped me in this project. In addition to our weekly classes, we are given assignments on various subjects. Each assignment requires that we write five-hundred-word essays. We read them during class, and they are critiqued by the teacher and discussed with the whole class. I hope this memoir indicates some level of my skills. Regardless, the class is an enjoyable three hours each Monday morning. Another four-hour period is required for writing the essay for the coming week.

Traveling so much in my working life, as recorded herein, makes staying at home enjoyable, even if I am alone. Each summer I promise myself that I am going to leave southern Louisiana to escape the July heat. I did so for two years. I flew to visit friends in Milwaukee in July 2006 and in 2007 I flew to visit a cousin, Phil, and his wife Dodo in Grand Junction, Colorado, located so far west that it is almost in Utah. For Christmas 2007 I flew to San Antonio to spend the holiday with Bill and Juanita. In 2008, Phil and Dodo visited with me during the spring. Now, using the shortage of gasoline as an excuse, I have decided to stay at home and let the crowds have the roadways and airlines, which are just too crowded during the holidays.

The Louisiana Honor Flight for WW II veterans from Lafayette to Washington D.C. to view the World War II memorial that had been built in our honor is a trip I shall never forget! Almost a thousand veterans, a hundred at a time, from the area made the trip, sponsored by the Lafayette community foundation. The foundation is a donor-focused philanthropic entity that exists to enhance the quality of life for its residents. They certainly honored the WW II veterans with an unforgettable trip we all shall remember. I was one of one hundred or so veterans who left on a Saturday morning for the round-trip flight to Washington. Some who went had never been on an airplane before. Leaving Lafayette Regional Airport was the first of many highlights. The waiting area was filled with family and friends who had come to see us off. Marine Corps Reserve members, in their dress blue uniforms, lined the walkway to the second-floor entrance of the airport and saluted each veteran as we entered. They held their salute for the entire group as we boarded the airplane. What a humbling feeling that was!

When we reached Reagan National Airport in Washington, a fire truck saluted us spraying a water cannon over the bow of the airplane. Then, as we entered the airport, we were cheered by two hundred or more people who waved American flags welcoming us. Walking to our buses, others applauded as if we had just won WW II. It brought tears to my eyes that people remembered the war and the sacrifices so many brave Americans had made.

In Washington, we boarded three buses—red, white, or blue so designated for each veteran by the color of the caps we were given. From there we drove almost all the way to the WW II memorial. Crowds were everywhere. Getting close to the memorial without a permit was impossible. We, therefore, walked the last bit, almost a mile, to the WW II memorial, where we were met by our Louisiana congressmen and congresswoman: Senator Mary Landrieu, with Representatives Charles Melancon and Charles Boustany. Also waiting was former senator Bob Dole, who attracted a crowd. The former senator had pictures taken with many of our comrades. The visit to the memorial was spectacular, as it was built at the end of the mall between the Lincoln Memorial and the Washington Monument. We also visited the Vietnam, Korean, and U.S. Marine Memorials. The Marine Memorial was outstanding and brought back memories of its origin, raising the flag on Iwo Jima's Mount Suribachi in 1945. Another highlight was the visit to the Tomb of the Unknown Solider at Arlington National Cemetery, where our group placed a wreath on the tomb. We also witnessed the changing of the guard, which brought back memories of life in the army.

The trip home was uneventful until we landed in Lafayette and were met by a crowd of five-hundred or more locals, complete with a local band playing at full blast.

Each of us was escorted down the second-floor escalator by a reserve corps U.S. Marine in full dress blues. This welcome made me feel as if I had won WW II single-handedly! It was a rewarding trip one in which I hope all veterans of the "big war" have an opportunity to take. It is sad that all survivors of our many other wars cannot be recognized as we were. The organizers of this trip are to be complimented for their thoughtfulness. I did so with a contribution. What a wonderful tribute that was!

Much time has passed since Rita left this earth. I have to find things to do to keep myself busy. For entertainment, I attend an occasional musical presentation in Lafayette, and a few movies. Eating out is another enjoyable event. Other times I find myself engaged with the computer. I also assist in administrating my mother's family's one-thousand-acre plantation in southern Louisiana. We lease the property for sugarcane farming and have recently leased 320 acres which we hope will produce oil and gas wells. Wells in other areas are drying up because they have been producing for more than twenty years. My three cousins and I are handling the day-to-day operations, which are not too time-consuming. I am chairman, and the others are filling the positions of treasurer and vice chairman. We hold an annual each September where we plan for the coming year. The meeting includes discussion of the past year's activities and approval of the next year's annual budget. The funds are usually divided among the twenty owners scattered over the United States. It keeps me busy about a month or two each year. Each year we discuss the need for hiring younger officers, since we are now all retired seniors. We do have four youngsters attending our meetings, who are known as "the futures"—all sons or daughters of active owners. We want them to become more acquainted with the operation of the property than we were when we took over in 2002, when our great uncle Cola died. He had been the sole manager for years.

TV and sporting events occupy some of my free time. I do enjoy football, baseball, golf events, a little basketball, and the news of the world. For much of 2007 and 2008, I was interested in politics for the presidential election in November 2008. Politicians are so long-winded. I hope that the preliminaries can be shortened to a few months rather than the year or longer period that it is now.

Sharing these memories has been an interesting project for me. It has brought back many good memories and many sad ones. My life with Rita was a most beautiful and memorable one. As I have said before, I have already spent my time in heaven on earth with her. It was a great life! My sincere hope is, and I do believe it is true, that she enjoyed it as much as I did. The memories discussed herein are those I shall never forget. If every married life could be as fortunate and loveable and wonderful as ours was, I know there would be fewer divorces in the world.

Rita was indeed the best thing that ever happened to me, and I look forward to the day when I meet her in heaven!